Sandy Lemmon,
Stay safe from all dogs.

Horton Kennedy

Preparing Yourself *for* Dog ENCOUNTERS

How to Handle Threats from Dogs and Defend Yourself against Dog Attacks:

THE FIRST COMPLETE, STEP-BY-STEP GUIDE TO PREVENTING DOG BITES

by

Hector L. Hernandez

Civilian Police-Dog Instructor

> This book presents in detail the most accurate information about preventing dog bites. It is a must for all those who encounter dogs as part of their employment, as well as for everyone who owns a dog or has contact with dogs, especially families with children.

FIRST CLASS
DOG TRAINING

Preparing Yourself
for
Dog
ENCOUNTERS

How to Handle Threats from Dogs
and Defend Yourself against
Dog Attacks

DEDICATION

This book is dedicated to all the victims of dog bites, especially the ones who lost their lives.

ISBN Print Ed. (10 digit) 0-9772220-0-4 (13 digit) 9780977222001

Cover Design and Book Layout
Infinity Graphics
2277 Science Pkwy, Ste. 5
Okemos, Michigan 48864
www.infinitygraphics.com

ABOUT THE AUTHOR

Photo by Brianna Hernandez, age 4

Hector L. Hernandez is a civilian police-dog trainer for various police agencies, in the State of Michigan. He has been training dogs for over twenty years and has been recognized as one of the best trainers in the United States for the protection phase of police dog, K9 training. In protection training, he uses the dog's instinct to protect its owner/handler, while at the same time encouraging the dog to maintain its positive, trusting relationship with humans. This is a major contribution to protection dog training.

Also, he regularly conducts obedience classes for dog owners and their dogs and also gives private lessons. He notes, with customary humor, "The dogs are easy; the owners are harder." Memorable and effective, his classes and individual training sessions leave both owner and dog with a long-lasting relationship of respectful obedience and mutual affection. He solves problems with dogs and their owners in a way which leaves you in awe of his ability to know how much to do to change bad behavior and when to back off and "let the dog teach itself." He understands that there are bad dogs/good owners and good dogs/bad owners, although most cases are at neither extreme. Both owners and dogs "just need to learn the concept," he will say at the beginning of a series of lessons.

He will not refuse any dog or owner, no matter how bad the relationship has become. Nor does he shy away from telling an owner the truth about the dog's (and owner's) problems. Sometimes these problems can't be solved; more often, with patience, they can.

His seminar/demonstrations for various groups of professionals and business people teach them how to prepare for dog encounters. In these sessions, he teaches a wide range of people from parents to fire fighters to animal shelter personnel how to protect themselves in dangerous situations with dogs. He demonstrates how "reading the dog's body language" can tell you the difference between a harmless encounter and a potentially dangerous one, and what to do about each situation. His speaking technique will make you laugh, while also making you think seriously about dog behavior and how to stay safe in all kinds of dog encounters. His chapter "for Kids" in *How to Prepare Yourself for Dog Encounters* should be must reading for every parent and grandparent.

His training programs have been accredited by the Michigan Commission on Law Enforcement Standards, and he is an evaluator for the American Kennel Club's "Canine Good Citizen" program. He served in the United States Marine Corps, receiving an Honorable Discharge in 1994.

He lives in Michigan with his wife Laura and two daughters, Brianna and MaLina. They share their home with their five dogs: Yorkshire Terrier Chula, Labrador Retriever Maggie and German Shepherds Tootsie, Tinkerbelle and Saint, as well as Ziggy the cat. He is also author of a forthcoming book, *How to Train Your Dog before Your Dog Trains You.*

A C K N O W L E D G E M E N T S

Gretchen Foster, editor, to whom I am greatly indebted. Without her this book would not have been written. She has patiently worked with me and tolerated my constant changes and additions.

Rick Foster, for his advice and support.

Karina Sa Leitao, editor.

Sgt. Mike Yankowski, Lansing Police Department K-9 Commander.

Sgt. Matt Maroni, Michigan State University Department of Public Safety K-9 Unit.

Sgt. Rick Hetu and Trooper Dave Yount, Michigan State Police K-9 Unit.

Mike Coplen, TASER International, Communications Department.

Commanding Officer Lt. Fegate, Los Angeles Police Department, Continuing Education Division.

Joel Hernandez, my brother, for being there with his advice.

Celia Hernandez, my sister, for her support.

Barb Beers, Assistant Trainer and reviewer of this book.

Pam Monaghan, Lansing Psychological Association P.C.

Maria Stephens, for getting me started with the post office seminars.

Jeanette McDougall, for her help on the groomer section.

Valerie Lee, for her advice about the parent section.

Clyde Smith, friend.

Dr. Mary T. Seager, DVM, for her advice about the veterinarians' section.

WJR 760 A.M. "News Talk," Detroit, Michigan. Listening to your station for countless hours has made me a better speaker. And National Public Radio, for the same reason.

Most of all, to my wife, Laura, who has picked up the slack for me countless times while I stayed up nights and buried myself on weekends writing this book. Laura, your unconditional love has made me a better husband and dog trainer. I realize every day what a fine choice I made when I said, "I do."

CONTENTS

—

PREFACE

How this book came into being

In April of 2004, I learned about a post office letter carrier that was bitten. I had asked another carrier if, since she had been working, she or her fellow letter carriers had received any training on preventing dog bites. She said, "We do, but it was not that good. All they show us is how a dog bites. She [the person giving the demonstration] does not go in detail about what to do." This lack of proper training is confirmed by the large number of letter carriers who are still getting bitten.

I searched the internet, but it gave me minimal information about preventing dog bites for those who encounter dogs as part of their employment and no information about what to do if you're attacked. There was a lot of advice from people, and some of that advice I read made me think that the dog was justified in biting those people. Some of these people giving advice had a dog that bit a protective arm, after which they explained what the dog did. But just seeing a dog biting a fake arm isn't enough. People who encounter potentially dangerous dogs need a step-by-step guide on what to do when a dog threatens or attacks them.

I began this book as a two-page brochure and proposed it to Maria Stephens from the U. S. Postal Service in Lansing, Michigan. Maria then proposed it to the Safety Committee. Two weeks later, I received a phone call to do four dog-encounter seminars. The day after the seminars, I started receiving e-mails and phone calls from attendees telling me how the seminars had already assisted them. At the very least, it made them feel confident about their next dog encounter. The word of mouth spread, and I started giving seminars at other post offices. While doing the seminars, I got many questions about what to do in other situations such as running, biking or preventing kids from getting bitten.

I started doing more research and again found very minimal advice about preventing dog bites in a variety of situations from running, to fire fighting, cycling, dog grooming, and many others. This was a topic I had a lot of experience in and loved to talk about, especially if it was going to help others. I knew I had to expand my pamphlet for letter carriers into a book for just about everyone.

Further search for books already written on this topic surprised me; there was not one book in the U.S.A. about how to prevent a dog bite or attack for working people who encounter dogs. Yet research from the Centers for Disease Control as well as my own experience told me that millions of people get bitten every year and millions of dollars are spent every year on lawsuits and medical bills. This made it even more urgent to write this book.

The most challenging sections were the ones for parents and kids and the one for law enforcement officers. I have written and rewritten these to make them as complete and understandable as I could. For parents and kids, the directions had to be clear and appropriate for both adults and kids to prevent vulnerable kids from getting bitten. The law enforcement section had to be written to conform with established police procedures and still protect officers from getting bitten and save dogs from being shot unnecessarily. For all the various groups, I consulted local practitioners in the field and incorporated their suggestions wherever possible.

A note on my use of male and female pronouns: When I started writing this book, I decided to alternate between using female and male pronouns instead of using the awkward "he/she, him/her" format. I believe this makes the text easier to read, and I hope as you read this book you will keep in mind that the situations I am describing can involve either a male or a female. When I say that "the owner should watch her dog's behavior," I do not imply that only a woman may be a dog owner or that a particular experience happens to women more than men. It's just my way of dealing with a dilemma that the English language presents.

Seminars

I am continuing to offer seminars to various groups whose jobs or ordinary lives involve encounters with dogs. These seminars will prepare you to respond confidently during a dog encounter. They range from 30 minutes to four hours depending on the group and the number of topics covered. I give hands-on demonstrations that will assist you to visualize and remember what you have learned. I also dispel the various myths about handling dogs and give you clear expectations for future encounters.

I have over 20 years of experience in the field of dog aggression and am a paid speaker and consultant for police agencies in the Mid-Michigan area. My expertise is in real street work, training police dogs, and I have been present on several occasions when deadly force had to be used during dog encounters. I take what I teach very seriously, but I use humor and lots of personal contact to get my message across.

Seminar attendees have said, "Hector Hernandez is guaranteed to be the best speaker, with the most update accurate information."

Since I began conducting Dog Encounter Seminars, I have received weekly phone calls about the progress people have made avoiding dog bites in their daily work.

To schedule a seminar:

If you or someone you know is interested in a seminar on how to prepare for dog encounters, check my web page ***www.firstclassdogtraining.com*** for details, including fees, travel expenses and other arrangements.

Readers' feedback

I look forward to your suggestions and feedback. They are very important to me. If the information in the book prevented you from getting bitten, or if you have suggestions about how to improve this book, please contact me through my website e-mail address:

www.firstclassdogtraining.com

*Check the website for forthcoming videos
showing how those addressed in each chapter of this book
can handle dog encounters.*

INTRODUCTION

According to the Centers for Disease Control:

- ☐ Every 40 seconds, someone in the United States seeks medical attention for a dog-bite related injury.
- ☐ Between 1979-1998, dog attacks killed more than 300 Americans.
- ☐ Nearly 800,000 people sought medical care for dog bites in 1994; half of them were children under 18.[1]

The cost of dog bites is equally dramatic. The CDC found that in 1994 "hospital charges for persons with dog bites totaled $40.5 million." The hospital charges do not include doctors' fees for in-hospital care, aftercare and treatment in emergency rooms. Adding all these costs together, one group of doctors estimated that total dog-bite related costs in 1994 came to $164.9 million.[2]

Most of us encounter dogs everyday either as part of our jobs or as private citizens. We don't think about the danger or cost of getting bitten or of having one of our kids get bitten. Certainly not every encounter with a dog will prove dangerous, but you need to know how to tell which encounters may be dangerous and which will not. I learned the hard way.

At the age of ten, I saw my neighbor's dog, a black and tan German Shepherd, lying in the front yard. I was so happy to see it, I started to pet it. As I tried to kiss it, it bit me right in the face. I jumped back startled, thinking, "Why did this dog bite me? Doesn't it know that I like it?" What was more confusing was that I had just seen the owners kiss it and play with it, and it seemed so happy.

After that I became curious about what makes dogs bite and how to tell if they're going to bite. My brother Joel, the same year, got our first dog, Max, a male, red Doberman Pinscher. Max did more than protect my family. He taught me the beginning of dog body language that still directs my thinking. I saw Max at his best and at his worst. I vividly remember what his body language did in all those behaviors. I saw Max at his best when I was throwing sticks in the water and having him bring them back to me, and also when he was protecting my house by barking. I saw him at his worst while I was handling him during protection training. The body language I learned from Max at his best and worst still directs my thinking and has taught me to respond quickly and accurately to behavior problems in all kinds of dogs. I spent every moment studying him, bonding with him and working with my brother to train Max. This helped keep me out of trouble with my peers on the city streets.

My brother and I trained Max in obedience using old traditional methods of force because at that time we didn't know any better way. I attended a protection class the year

---

[1] CDC website: *www.cdc.gov/ncipc/fact_book/14_Dog_Bite_Injuries.htm.* 1/27/2005.

[2] CDC website: *www.cdc.gov/duip/hospital.htm.* The CDC cites various studies published in the *Journal of the American Medical Association* in 1988 together with a report to Congress in 1989 on "Cost of Injury in the United States," conducted by the University of California and Johns Hopkins.

after we got Max. The instructor used kicks, pinching and pulling of the flanks and slaps to the face to get the dogs to be aggressive. The training did make Max aggressive, but it also made him fearful and very unpredictable.

After the first protection class, I became hooked. I started learning protection training. I would tease the dog to get a reaction to my behavior. I quickly learned that my behavior determined the dog's behavior. I refused to use any force to make a dog aggressive. I learned that force was a brutal shortcut used by individuals who either didn't know what they were doing or were impatient. I learned my own style, using only body language to make the dog react in an aggressive or friendly way.

I learned how to trigger a confrontation or a dog bite by adapting the dog's aggressive body language to human body language. Understanding how dogs communicate through their body language allows us to communicate with them using our own body language in place of words.

By mimicking dogs' body language, we become aware of what dogs see as a threat, a challenge, play, submission and incitement to a fight. We learn to recognize these body language signals in dogs to avoid getting bitten and prepare ourselves for a potentially dangerous encounter with a dog. You will find these described from the dog's point of view in the chapters that follow in the final sections, "How to understand a dog's body language." Here are ways humans can copy dogs in each body language signal:

| *Threatening body language* | *Challenging body language* | *Playful body language* | *Submissive body language* | *Retreat* |

☐ **Threat** — moving slowly, enter the dog's space with direct eye contact.

☐ **Challenge** — standing your ground, lean your entire body forward with your arms out.

☐ **Play** — moving side to side and bouncing while approaching low.

☐ **Submission** — turning your head away, crouch down with your back turned away from the dog.

☐ **Retreat** — turning your back, signals to the dog it has won. Making you vulnerable to be bitten by giving confidence to a dog.

☐ **Incitement to a fight** — charging repeatedly at the dog with your body stiff and looking directly at the dog's eyes.

Your body language can also mimic a dog's natural prey and lead to a bite or even a kill. Here are the main ways to show you are a dog's prey:

- ☐ Move close to the dog, stop and run away.
- ☐ Run away making a high-pitched noise — scream or yell.
- ☐ Show the dog a threatening or challenging behavior and then run away.

I have used these kinds of body language to train dogs to be aggressive. For example, I would slowly approach while moving furtively as if I were about to do something bad, then make quick movements. I would either run away or stand my ground, facing the dogs. If I wanted to trigger a bite, I would invade the dog's personal space, wait for an aggressive response and continue forward, moving closer to the dog's face and present the bite sleeve (a fake arm made from a burlap covered cylinder), while simultaneously turning my back to retreat.

To convey to a dog that I was not a threat, I would walk towards it in a relaxed manner, taking slow deep breaths, with my mouth open. While approaching the dog, I would look at it but not stare into its eyes. As I got closer, I would stop, call its name in a soft voice, and then call it to me or have the handler bring it to me.

By 1986, I started working with local police agencies. At that time, the police did not purchase trained dogs, so they had to be taught from ground zero. They were usually donated by private citizens or animal shelters. I quickly became a regular at the police agencies' training and re-training days. I preferred working with dogs from ground zero because I could mold them the way I wanted them. I always teach the "friends" command to police dogs, because that allows the dog to trust people, something that is very difficult to train if the dog is already trained to bite people. I learned early on that it's much easier to train a dog to dislike certain human behavior than to train it to like a certain behavior. So, choosing a dog that likes people is vital to its being a good patrol dog and public relations tool.

In 1991, the Michigan State University K-9 Unit certified me as a Police K-9 Instructor. Since then, I have worked with various other agencies. I have attended and instructed at countless seminars in my specialty, protection training.

Training dogs in police work, especially protection, has given me the experience to read the dog's body language. The years I spent learning to read dogs' body language and studying their aggression have given me the knowledge to write this book. In my opinion, protection training is the most important facet of police work with dogs. In the course of such work, whenever a dog bite occurs, the dog's training is at stake. And the police department's liability is in question, so the training must be as perfect as possible.

Understanding how to balance a dog's aggression with obedience and switching the dog's aggressive behavior on and off by body language alone constitute a fine art. I have spent over half my life training and studying dogs. During all my years of training, I have been seriously bitten only three times. All were due to handler error. My last serious bite was in March, 2004, at a national seminar in Florida. I received a ten-inch bite and tooth drag on the rear-end. While writing this book I was constantly reminded how I don't want anyone feeling what I felt — my body going numb with pain and not being able to think clearly during and after the bite.

The alarming truth is that millions of people get bitten every year, and some even die. I want this book to train people how to prepare themselves to avoid or deal with dog threats, especially kids and families. I want all the different kinds of people who read this book to benefit from what I have learned. Then they can prepare for every dog encounter they will face and avoid getting bitten, as I should have done when I was 10.

The professionals for whom this book will be especially useful include law enforcement officers, firemen and women, post office workers, utility service personnel, cyclists, runners, delivery personnel, veterinarians, groomers, home care visitors, and the personnel at animal shelters, humane societies and dog adoption centers. While some chapters in this book are specifically designed for these groups, virtually all those whose jobs require that they encounter dogs can benefit from this book. These include people who deliver telephone books and newspapers door to door, census workers, political canvassers and many others. You will find many useful tips on dealing with dogs in the chapters for "Delivery Personnel," "Home Care Workers," even the one for "Runners, Joggers, Skaters and Walkers."

Above all, I hope parents and their children will read this carefully. I suggest that you play "pretend dog encounter" with your kids, using stuffed animals, to help them remember what they should do if a dog threatens them.

For what to do during a dog encounter or attack, I have provided checklists of recommended behaviors and boxes to check off as you work through them. You may wish to make your own shortlist of what you need to do most often in your particular circumstances, but don't ignore the suggestions for things that may not yet have happened but could happen sometime. Your future welfare could depend on how ready you are to handle all aspects of a potentially dangerous dog encounter. Learn about what makes dogs do what they do. Stay safe.

Getting started:

Each Section has several options which will help you defend yourself against a dog encounter, each option is a reaction to the dog's behavior towards you. Initially, when reading them you may be overwhelmed with all the choices. But, when encountered by a dog, you will understand why there are several options. One option may not work for a particular dog but may for another. Choose one or more options that you feel the most comfortable with and utilize them. However, don't disregard the others as you may need them if your choice fails to work. Remember, some of these suggestions may work to deter one particular dog but not another; or an option may work on a dog one day but the same option may not work on the same dog another day. Remember that you have no idea what the dog's past experiences with other people have been like and those past experiences could have an effect on how the dog will respond to you. A dog's behavior can change very quickly and you must be prepared when it does. So, review your options from time to time to refresh your memory.

LEGAL MATTERS

Leash laws:

Most cities, counties and states have leash laws which specifically require dogs to be under control and on a leash on public property. Even if your city or state does not have such laws, it would be in your best interest to leash your dog when it is off your property.

Having your dog under control when on leash requires some training. The leash alone is not sufficient. Even though it restrains the dog from moving freely, a dog can still bite someone when on leash. Leash laws establish many safety measures. They help prevent dog bites, having your dog injured by a car or a person, spreading diseases and the possibility of your dog's becoming a member of a pack which may then attack people.

No matter how well trained your dog is, the dog is still a dog. The chance that your dog will be distracted and led into danger through its instincts is still present. Squirrels, rabbits, cats, dogs or people playing with toys (balls, Frisbees) could distract your dog long enough for it to be hit by a car or bite someone out of fun or aggression.

If your dog damages other people's property or hurts or kills someone, you are liable. You, as the owner, are responsible for your dog's behavior; your dog cannot be sued. Fines vary from state to state. If you violate the leash law or allow your dog to be out of control and damage other people or their property, you, not your dog, will pay the fine or other penalty.

Warning about encountering police dogs:

The advice about striking an attacking dog does not apply to police dogs. If you try to hit a trained police dog, it will fight harder and hold onto you more firmly. Police dogs receive hundreds of hours of training in catching and holding criminals so that the police officers using them can control the dogs under conditions that occur on the street. Police dogs are trained to release their hold if pain is inflicted on them and then re-engage with another target.

If you fight against a police dog, you may well cause its tunnel vision to take over, making it more difficult for the police officer to call the dog off. Furthermore, the officers will not stand by and watch you strike their dogs. They are trained to fight alongside the dog to apprehend criminals, if necessary. In most states, it is unlawful to molest or kill a police dog. If you do so, the pain you experience from the police dog's bite will be enhanced by the pain of legal penalties.

Fines and penalties will be levied based on what has been done to the police dog. In most states, teasing or molesting a police dog starts with a misdemeanor charge, leading up to a year in jail and a fine of up to $1,000. If you cause the death of a police dog, you will be charged with a felony and receive up to three years in prison and a fine for restitution of the dog. The average police dog costs over $10,000.

Warning about using a firearm against an attacking dog:

If you find yourself in a situation where you think you need to use a firearm against a dog, before trying to use it, call the police or notify someone else to call them if time and circumstances permit. You must exercise caution when using a firearm against a dog that is attacking you or someone else.

If a police officer arrives at the scene and doesn't see the dog, he may think you are pointing the firearm at a person, especially if the person being attacked by the dog is yelling and waving her arms while you are pointing the weapon at the dog. If that person is a police officer or is armed, he may shoot at you, thinking you are trying to shoot another person. Furthermore, if you do discharge the weapon, the bullet may ricochet and hit someone else, causing severe injury or even death.

How federal law views defending a dog against injury up to death:

If a person injures or kills a dog, even if the dog is doing no harm, you are not justified in exercising lethal force against that person. Under federal law, a dog is a piece of property, not a person. (*Dye v Wargo*, 253 F. 3d 296 (2001) Seventh Circuit). You may not use deadly force to protect property (*Tennessee v Garner*, 471 US 1, 85 L Ed 2d 1, 105 S Ct. 1694 (1985)).

If deadly force used against a dog escalates to deadly force against you, then using deadly force against the person attacking you may be justified (*Mettler v Whitledge*, 165 F. 3d 1197, Eighth Circuit (1999)).

Michigan dog law:

Residents of states other than Michigan should check with their states' laws regarding dangerous animals and dogs.

Michigan statute details: citation from M.C.L.A. 287.321:

Sec. 1. As used in this act: "Dangerous animal" means a dog or other animal that bites or attacks and causes serious injury or death to another dog while the other dog is on the property or under the control of its owner. However a dangerous animal does not include any of the following:

An animal that bites or attacks a person who is knowingly trespassing on the property of the animal's owner.

An animal that bites or attacks a person who provokes or torments the animal.

An animal that is responding in a manner that an ordinary and reasonable person would conclude was designed to protect a person if that person is engaged in a lawful activity or is the subject of an assault.

****

"Owner" means a person who owns or harbors a dog or other animal.

"Provoke" means to perform a willful act or omission that an ordinary and reasonable person would conclude is likely to precipitate the bite or attack by an ordinary dog or animal.

"Serious injury" means permanent, serious disfigurement, serious impairment of health, or serious impairment of a bodily function of a person.

****

(f) "Torment" means an act or omission that causes unjustifiable pain, suffering, and distress to an animal, or causes mental and emotional anguish in the animal as evidenced by its altered behavior, for a purpose such as sadistic pleasure, coercion, or punishment that an ordinary and reasonable person would conclude is likely to precipitate the bite or attack.

Dog owner's liability:

In addition to being subject to civil liability, the owner of a dangerous dog that kills a person is guilty of involuntary manslaughter. An involuntary manslaughter conviction carries up to 15 years imprisonment, a fine of up to $77,500, or both.

The owner of a dangerous dog that attacks a person and causes serious injury other than death, is guilty of a felony punishable by up to four years imprisonment, a fine not less than $2,000, community service work for not less than 500 hours, or any combination of these penalties. Serious injury means a permanent, serious disfigurement, serious impairment of health, or serious impairment of a bodily function.

If an animal was previously found to be dangerous and the dog attacks a person and causes an injury that is not serious, the owner is guilty of a misdemeanor, punishable by imprisonment of not more than 90 days, a fine up to $500, community service work for not less than 240 hours, or any combination of these penalties.

PREPARING YOURSELF
FOR DOG ENCOUNTERS FOR:

PARENTS

(Written for the Love and Safety of our Children)

—

Bites from family dogs account for a large percentage of the bites that lead to serious injuries. It's vital to teach your kids not to think every dog is their friend and should be trusted. Kids think that their dog will like their friends the same way it likes them and will respond to their friends' petting and playing with it in the same way it does to them. Unfortunately, this is not true for dogs. A family dog has no commitment to kids outside its family pack, nor does it see them as members of that pack. The dog doesn't know these outside kids are its owner's friends or relatives. Your kids must learn that their friends won't necessarily be able to interact with their dog the same way they do. The dog's owners will have to introduce kids outside their family to their dog gradually and in a controlled, obedience situation. Only time will make the dog trust kids not in its family.

Paul, Laura, Amber 12, Austin 9, Kyle 7 with Akira and Sabra

After reading this chapter, all parents should read the next chapter for "Kids" with their children and talk about what the kids should do in a scary dog encounter.

Selecting the right dog for your family:

☐ Research the breed and breeder (see *How to Train Your Dog before Your Dog Trains You,* "Picking the Pick of the Litter and the Right Kind of Breeder"[3]).

☐ Estimate size and energy level when full grown.

☐ Consider your life style and the temperaments of all your family members.

☐ Decide how much time you can devote to exercising the dog.

☐ Test the puppy or dog for any signs of aggression.

Who is targeted for getting bitten, and how do bites occur?

Young children are the main targets. Between 1979-1998, the Centers for Disease Control tracked dog bites and bite-related deaths. They concluded: "Children are at greater risk of injury and death from dog bites. Many children do not know how to behave around a dog. Children's small size and inability to fend off an attack may put them at additional risk."[4] Twice as many children as adults get bitten. From 1979-1998, 27 people died as a result of dog bites, and 19 were children under the age of 15.

Young children (ages 5-9) have the highest rate of emergency-room visits for dog bites, and boys get bitten oftener than girls. Most bites to children occur on the face, head and neck, and children under 10 receive 65 percent of the bites to the face. Contrary to what you would think, strange dogs are not doing the biting. Two-thirds of the bites occur at the child's home from a dog the child knows. Breeds at the highest risk for biting are in descending order: Pit Bulls, Rottweilers, German Shepherds, Siberian Huskies, Alaskan Malamutes, Doberman Pinschers, Chows, Great Danes, St. Bernards and Akitas. However, the popularity of specific breeds adds to the increase in that breed's documented bites. This popularity is sure to change from time to time, and with it the frequency of bites for the various breeds. Key facts you should keep in mind:

☐ Most of the bite victims are children under 10 years old.

☐ They get bitten on the head and face by dogs that are owned by their families, relatives and friends because kids try to hug and kiss them.

☐ Most dog bites occur in the afternoon and evening and are more frequent from March to September, probably because kids are playing more with dogs outside after school and during the warm months.

☐ Dog bites peak in July when kids are on vacation.

☐ Others at risk for getting bitten are injured, sick, old and weak adults.

---

[3] Hector L. Hernandez, 2005.

[4] For information about dog bites in the U.S., I am indebted to the Centers for Disease Control's website: *www.cdc.gov/ncipc/fact_book/14_Dog_Bite_Injuries.htm.* 1/27/2005.

☐ Newborn babies get bitten by dogs with high prey drives and killing instincts.

☐ The bites from family dogs usually occur while petting, rough playing or startling the dog while it is sleeping.

☐ Stray dogs will usually bite on the legs, because people turn and walk or run away instead of facing the dog and backing away.

☐ Bites on the hands and arms occur when the victims put up their hands and arms for protection. Dogs learn to bite at kids' hands and arms through playing with them and seeing their moving hands and arms as the human version of a dog's mouth. With another dog they bite at the mouth; with humans they bite at hands and arms.

Underground electric fence containment systems:

If you have an underground electric containment fence, don't rely on it as a secure way to confine your dog all day. Your dog may not leave the yard, but other dogs and children will have easy access to the area. Plus there is always the possibility that your dog will cross the fence boundary. Some dogs can work themselves into such an aggressive state that they break through the boundary, numb to the shock, to attack a dog or person. Also, in order to insure that you receive your mail and other home deliveries, keep the boundary as far away as possible from any delivery access, including mail boxes.

Newborn babies and dogs:

The most tragic incident is when a dog kills or maims a newborn. Although such attacks are infrequent, you should know how to protect your newborn just in case a threat arises. When you bring a newborn baby home for the first time, your dog will have no clue that it is part of your family. It will view the newborn as someone else entering the pack and see that the new pack member is weak and vulnerable. A nurse in the hospital where my last child was born told me to take home one of my newborn's blankets containing its scent for my dog to smell. Although this may be good advice to introduce the family dog to a new human smell, it has little or no connection to the dog's actual meeting with the newborn or to the dog's reaction to the baby when it is crying and appearing vulnerable.

Before introducing the newborn, you want to evaluate your dog's temperament and also look for any change in its behavior when faced with new people or kids. Does the dog have a dominant personality? If it does, it may test its new pack member when the leader is not around. Does the dog have a killing instinct? If so, the dog could mistake the baby's cry for a death scream (such as animals release during distress or before death), inducing it to attack a motionless, vulnerable newborn. Or does the dog have a history of being nervous or fearful around new people, kids and newborns? If it does, then most likely it will be nervous and fearful around the newborn, the newest pack member. Fear and nervousness lead to unpredictability, causing the dog to display aggression. Understanding your dog's behavior is far more vital than allowing it to smell the newborn's blanket.

Tips on introducing a dog to a newborn and keeping the baby safe:

Have a professional trainer evaluate your dog's temperament for signs of fear or killing instinct. Know your dog's weaknesses and what it does when those weaknesses are tested: pull on ears, skin and tail; touch feet; poke nose and eyes. Does your dog tolerate this, get up and move, or bite? Never trust your dog alone with a newborn. It may not bite, but it could play with the baby roughly enough to hurt it. The dog might walk over the baby, play bite hard enough to cause injury or even lick it too much, causing panic to the newborn.

In the worst case, your dog could bite the baby seriously. Train your dog not to jump on you; newborns have been knocked away from parents' arms by jumping dogs. Continue to evaluate your dog's behavior as your baby starts to crawl and walk. Both stages indicate to your dog that the baby is injured and thus vulnerable. This could lead to a bite.

Certain breeds about which to be cautious:

Certain breeds that were originally bred for fighting and guarding are difficult to read. Because they have been selectively bred not to display any signs of aggression prior to a fight or attack, you will have trouble anticipating their aggression. Right up to the time they attack, they will be silent, and their body language will not reveal their intent. For a discussion of these breeds see the chapter entitled "Dogs That Are Dangerous or Fighters, Because of Breeding or Learned Behavior."

Senior dogs:

Kids are at risk of getting bitten by senior dogs because they don't understand the physical and mental stress the aging dog may be experiencing. The dog's breed, diet, exercise and genetics contribute to how and when the signs of aging appear. In general, smaller dogs live longer than large ones. Smaller dogs are considered senior at about 11; large breeds, at about eight. Below are the reasons why older dogs bite and a list of some things to consider as your dog gets older:

Signs of aging are:

- ☐ Slowness in getting up from naps or sleep.
- ☐ Slowness going up and down stairs — stopping on each step and continuing this all the way down.
- ☐ Walking as if it were on ice or on a hot surface.
- ☐ Graying of hair on muzzle and around eyes.
- ☐ Beginning to withdraw from people and other pets — wanting to be alone.
- ☐ Sleeping longer and eating less, in some cases.

Causes of bites:

- ☐ Arthritis pain. This will make the dog irritable and less tolerant of being hung onto and pulled around by kids, even if the dog has allowed it in the past.

- ☐ Loss of vision and hearing — the dog will compensate for its lack of vision and hearing by becoming more alert and attuned to smells and vibrations around them, thus making the dog more nervous and easily startled. The dog will bite first and ask questions later.

- ☐ Not feeling good — have your veterinarian do a medical screening of your older dog to rule out any sickness.

Solutions for aggression in dogs:

Although no formal study has been done to connect obedience training with aggression, my experience with training dogs using the right method and taking the dog's personality into account indicates that obedience training is vital for preventing aggression as well as solving many forms of behavior problems. Below are some suggestions from my experience in solving aggression problems.

- ☐ Establish an obedience relationship with your dog before you establish an emotional one.

- ☐ Know your dog's temperament — its strengths and weaknesses.

- ☐ Channel the dog's instinct into forms of play or benefit from the dog's instinctive behavior by using it.

- ☐ Train the dog using the right method based on the dog's temperament.

- ☐ Start training as early as four months.

- ☐ Expose your dog to different environments and people.

- ☐ Don't rough play with dogs.

- ☐ Neuter or spay your dog.

- ☐ Make sure the dog is healthy.

- ☐ Pay attention to genetics before getting a dog. Find out if it's over-bred (mother had too many litters), in-bred or poorly bred.

How obedience training can help control aggression:

Obedience is not instinctive in dogs. When humans domesticated dogs, we had to learn how to train them so we could live side by side with them. Aggressive behavior in dogs is instinctive and is directly related to their survival. Dogs in the wild must protect themselves to stay alive. If a dog is allowed to be aggressive or is taught to be aggressive in protection training before it receives any training in obedience, the handler will have more difficulty controlling its behavior. The dog's aggressive instinct has surfaced, and the dog will then be free to choose how much aggression to display because it has received no training in how to control its behavior.

The solution to counteract aggression before it surfaces is to train the dog in obedience while it is still a puppy. Four months is the best time to start because at this age dogs begin to test their position in their pack (their human family), but they have not reached their full strength either physically or mentally. A dog's genetic purpose instincts will usually emerge between six and twelve months of age. Early obedience training will teach the dog that you are in charge so, if aggression emerges, you as the handler can decide how much, if any, is merited.

Obedience training will not remove the dog's aggressive instincts, but it will modify them so you can control your dog. It's vital to use the training method that is right for your particular dog's temperament. Dogs do not all think and behave the same way. The wrong training method can actually contribute to your dog's aggressiveness. In general, I do not recommend training with treats, because it makes the dog selfish and unaccountable for its mistakes. The treat method encourages a dog to become aggressive when it wants to. Most dogs can be successfully trained using a training chain, if the handler does it correctly. On passive dogs, however, a training chain can create fear, and the dog will show aggression out of its fear. For a complete discussion of how to train your dog see *How to Train Your Dog before Your Dog Trains You,* Hector L. Hernandez, 2005.

Even for trained police dogs, obedience training should come before protection training; otherwise the handler will have trouble getting the dog to release its bite on command and in general controlling its aggressive behavior.

Fearful dog behavior, and why fearful dogs are dangerous:

A fearful dog may be dangerous because its fear causes it to be unpredictable. Fear can drive the dog to escape by retreating. If cornered with no way out, such a dog will bite because of its survival instinct. Your kids don't know the dog's body language that signals fear. Often kids think a dog that is running away out of fear wants to play, and they will chase after it. If they corner the dog, and get too close (invade its personal space), the dog will probably bite.

Another dangerous situation occurs when the dog is lying down and your child tries to hug or kiss it. Again, the dog feels cornered and either can't escape or chooses not to move, so it will bite instead.

Giving love and praise to a fearful dog in the hope that your comfort will help it overcome its fear, doesn't work. In most cases, if you try to comfort a fearful dog by praising it, the dog's behavior will become worse, because it sees your comfort and touch as praise for being fearful. Your best option is to build your dog's confidence by training it in obedience. Then, when the dog becomes fearful, you can use obedience commands to enable the dog to control itself while it is afraid. The body language and behavior of a fearful dog are:

- ☐ eyes looking back and forth repeatedly
- ☐ mouth closed and tensed

- ☐ eyes wide open
- ☐ tail usually down, but could be in any position
- ☐ hair from the shoulder blades to the tail standing up
- ☐ ears either pulled back or pulled downward from their normal position
- ☐ could be barking
- ☐ could be running away.

Spoiled dog syndrome (SDS) and aggression:

The dog's owners create this problem when they give the dog continuous praise and love without the dog earning it by serving them in accord with its instinctual purpose in life. You spoil your dog when you allow it to sleep on your bed, treat it as if it were a human and fail to obedience train it using the right method.[5]

Your dog does not fulfill its instinctual purpose in life by serving your human emotional needs. If you shower emotional attention on your dog, you create frustration and misunderstanding in your dog. By trying to make it into a human, you spoil it as a dog. A spoiled dog will throw tantrums by becoming destructive and manipulative. It will release its stress by destroying anything that carries your scent: shoes, clothes, furniture, even remote controls, to name a few. It manipulates you by barking, pawing you to get what it wants or intimidating you by threatening to bite when it doesn't get its way. You might put up with the destructiveness and manipulation, but the consequences of its aggression (such as serious bites to people) can be devastating.

Your spoiled dog will start to view you as its property, claiming you by not allowing anyone to come near you and showing aggression to stop others from invading your space or its space. This space may increase over time to include your room, house or yard. In some cases, your dog will attempt to bite you while it's acting aggressive because its rage doesn't allow it to control itself. It may also try to bite you if you attempt to move it from its favorite place such as your lap or bed.

Your failure to train your dog will make it believe you are not its leader and will make the dog not accountable to anyone for its behavior. Once it understands that showing aggression toward you works, it may carry its aggression over to other people because it has learned that being aggressive is a good way to communicate with humans. This sets up a cycle of behavior in which the dog's aggressive behavior is rewarded by people when they show fear and retreat from it. When this happens, your spoiled dog becomes dangerous.

Nine kinds of aggressive behaviors:

If any dog shows aggression towards your children, remove the dog immediately. Do not use any child as a training aid, hoping the dog will get over its aggression. Dogs that

---

[5] See *How to Train Your Dog before Your Dog Trains You,* Hector L. Hernandez, 2005.

threaten children are a serious problem; seek advice from a professional dog trainer, preferably one who has extensive experience in managing dog aggression.

All of these types of aggressive behavior may trigger a dog bite:

- ☐ *Female aggressive behavior:* Protecting their puppies, because of female hormones, lack of socialization, improper training, false pregnancies and genetic predisposition.

- ☐ *Male aggressive behavior:* Testosterone, lack of socialization, improper training and genetic predisposition.

- ☐ *Aggressive behavior caused by fear:* A dog shows its fear-aggressiveness when it has its tail tucked under its belly, its body is tensed and its head and body are tucked in. It looks at you while moving its eyes back and forth, possibly showing its teeth as a warning that it feels cornered and is trying to escape because of its fear.

- ☐ *Aggressive behavior caused by pain:* Injury or low pain tolerance.

- ☐ *Aggressive behavior caused by dominance:* Uses body to push, demands attention with or without growls, has genetic predisposition to aggression, is being rough-played with by dogs or humans.

- ☐ *Aggressive behavior caused by predatory instincts:* Chases and/or attacks animals or things that are moving, has tunnel vision when it sees an animal or things that are moving, and exhibits stalking body language.

- ☐ *Aggressive behavior caused by possessiveness:* Growls or attempts to bite when near its toys or food. Keeps toys or objects near it, growling or attempting to bite when it is approached for fear of having its toys or food taken away from it. The object of its growls or bite could be human. See below for a full discussion of how to control food possessiveness.

- ☐ *Aggressive behavior caused by territorial instinct:* Barking and possibly attempting to bite at strangers and other dogs when its space is invaded. A dog that is tied up will claim and protect its territory as far as it can reach. A dog will see the territory bounded by the leash as its own. If your dog is barking at anyone invading its territory (letter carrier, delivery person) wait to open the door until the dog is calm or secure. If you open the door the dog may burst out chasing down the person, the person not expecting to be chased will not be prepared to defend himself and could get bitten.

- ☐ *Aggressive behavior caused by repressed instincts:* Not channeling the dog's natural instinct can cause it to become aggressive, because you have not replaced its instinct with a harmless outlet.

Food possessiveness and aggression:

Controlling a dog's possessiveness toward food is vital to maintaining order in the human family pack. With proper training and socializing, you can prevent your dog from becoming aggressively possessive about its food. Many good dogs do not pass the test of controlling their aggressiveness when eating because they are tested under conditions guaranteed to make the dog fail. These include testing the dog after it has been without food or is under stressful conditions at an animal shelter or other unfamiliar surroundings.

Before this test can be administered fairly, the dog must be in a stable condition with its basic needs fulfilled: food, shelter and medical care. In addition you need to be sure it has a chance to fulfill its instinctive purpose as a dog. See below for the section on "Helping your dog serve its purpose in life." It is unfair to the dog to interfere with its feeding if you haven't taken the time to teach it to control itself, because when you come between a dog and its food you are asking it not to follow its canine survival instincts. You are expecting it to act like a civilized human, not like a dog.

You can, however, modify your dog's aggressive behavior during feeding. If your dog succeeds in biting a child or adult during feeding, it is probably because they have not respected its feeding time. You should always supervise your children when the dog is eating. We demand a higher standard from dogs than we do from humans. As children, we have to be taught not to take food from other people's plates and not to bother them when they're eating. We must do the same for dogs.

Dogs learn food possessiveness as newborn puppies. The mother will usually have two parallel rows of five teats. At birth, puppies will fight and growl at one another when trying to get hold of a teat. This increases when there is a large litter with more puppies than teats. During the fight for their mother's milk, the weaker puppies will be forced to fight hard with the stronger ones if they want to survive. The stronger puppies will learn to fight to keep what they have. The longer the puppies stay in the litter, the more their food possessiveness will be reinforced. The fighting and growling carry over when the puppies are switched to solid food. The toughest puppy gets the most food by eating fast and growling to intimidate the others. The puppy will show the same growling and fighting behavior toward humans unless it learns early on that it doesn't have to fight humans for its food.

If your puppy or dog is possessive about its food, do not use physical or verbal correction. This will only add stress to the dog's behavior and give it no option but to fight for its food. It will help curb possessiveness if you remove empty food bowls from the floor. If you are free feeding (that is keeping food in the dog's bowl all the time), you will have a harder time teaching your dog not to be possessive about food. Free feeding removes the dog's dependence on its owner for food. The dog regards the human who brings it its food as its pack leader. By replacing the human food provider with an always full bowl, you may well teach your dog that the pack leader has no control over its food and it will become more possessive about its bowl and food. For this reason, I do not recommend free feeding.

You want to imprint on the dog's mind that it does not control the feeding ritual. You, as the top dog (or alpha) and as the leader of the family, control feeding and determine who eats first and who eats last. Here's how I recommend you feed your dog:

- ☐ Before feeding, have the food out so the dog can see it.
- ☐ Have the dog "sit" and "stay."
- ☐ Put its food down on the floor.
- ☐ If your dog breaks the "sit/stay" correct this disobedience verbally by saying, "No. Stay," and lift the food off the floor. Note that you are not correcting your dog's desire for the food; you are correcting its disobedience in breaking the "sit/stay."
- ☐ Make sure your dog is "staying," and replace the food on the floor.
- ☐ Give the command, "Okay, eat."
- ☐ If your dog growls or attempts to bite you during feeding, *do not* correct it for that.
- ☐ Instead, go directly to an obedience command, such as "sit," "down" or "stay."
- ☐ If you challenge your dog about being possessive over its food, it will have no choice but to fight back, as it learned to do in the litter and as its survival instinct tells it to do.

When your dog has mastered the "sit/stay" before feeding, try calling it away from the food to come to you. When the dog comes, give it a special treat such as cooked chicken or bacon, something your dog will love. Don't correct the dog if it doesn't come. This may be too much to ask. You can put your dog on a lead and pull it off its food, saying, "Come," and showing it the special treat.

Another method is to hand feed your dog from its bowl. Give it a handful of food at a time until the meal is complete. As the dog gets better at accepting your being near its food, with your other hand touch it before and after it eats each handful of food. Wait to touch your dog while it is eating when its behavior is relaxed and it shows no signs of aggression. If at any time, the dog starts to get aggressive by growling during hand feeding, close your hand and do not allow the dog to continue eating. Wait a few seconds, touch the dog again with your free hand and continue hand feeding.

Once the dog understands your presence as non-threatening, approach it with a treat until you can be next to the bowl dropping the treat in the bowl and touching the dog. Repeat dropping the treat and having your hand present until the dog is excited about your presence.

Stealing food from children:

When certain dogs want food they will assert their leadership position and take (steal) food from people. This can happen to adults, but children seem to be more vulnerable because the dog knows a child is weaker than an adult. Dogs may bite children who are carrying food; this occurs when the dog is attempting to steal the food from the child's hand.

The child can also be bitten if he resists the dog; the dog then tries harder, using aggression to win the challenge. If the dog does succeed in stealing the food and the child wants the food back, the dog then resorts to aggression again to keep the food. This is often confused with food possessiveness behavior, but instead it is an assertion of dominance.

To solve this problem, do the following:

- ☐ Control the dominance you observe through proper obedience training and exercises. Affirm your leadership without using forceful methods on the dog.
- ☐ Isolate the dog when the family is eating.
- ☐ Do not feed the dog from your hand; rather place all food in a bowl.
- ☐ Be cautious about using treats during training. This may give the dog the idea that it can take food from your hand (or anyone's hand). If your dog is treat-trained, understand that its food stealing could occur more often than otherwise.
- ☐ Don't allow children to walk around with food. This tempts the dog so strongly that even training will not modify its desire to take the food.

Medical intervention for aggressive behavior:

In most cases, the right method of obedience training is the foundation for solving all behavior problems, including aggression. If the dog has a medical condition, however, obedience training will not help. Such a condition can occur at any time in a dog's life. Before consulting a trainer about your dog's aggression, have your veterinarian evaluate it for a possible medical problem. Here are a few of the conditions that can make a dog aggressive; consult your veterinarian for a complete list: abnormally high or low thyroid secretions, hypoglycemia (low blood sugar), brain tumors, head trauma (head injury resulting in swelling or bleeding).

Puppies and dogs play-biting:

We must stop biting as early as possible. You must teach your puppy or dog that biting is not accepted. It's instinctive for dogs to bite other dogs in playing and mock fighting and defending themselves, but not to bite humans. When we remove a puppy from its litter and surround it with humans, a biting problem can arise. The puppy still wants to engage in play biting, so it transfers this behavior to humans. No matter what the circumstances, do not allow your puppy or dog to bite your clothes or skin. From the dog's point of view, your clothes are an extension of your skin, similar to its fur. We laugh when we see a cute puppy tugging at our shoe laces or pant legs, not realizing that the puppy will grow up with the idea that it's okay to bite. Letting your dog bite you or your clothes teaches it that such behavior is acceptable to humans.

Handling chewing and teething in puppies:

Chewing and teething come naturally to all dogs. Knowing when your dog starts teething and why it chews will help you prepare how to act before the dog does a lot of damage. Teething puppies will bite to relieve the itching and to loosen their teeth. Dogs have approximately 28 baby teeth that erupt before they are six weeks old. They start losing their baby teeth before they are six months old. Their back teeth, called the molars, start coming in at six to seven months. So it would be safe to say that dogs go through the teething process for eight months.

Most adult dogs have 42 teeth. Some dogs that have ears that stand up may lose ear strength while teething. This happens because most of their calcium is going to the teeth, leaving very little for other parts of the body. After teething, the calcium will become distributed more evenly. Some drooling may occur as a way of lubricating the gums. While your puppy is teething, chewing comes naturally, so you must puppy proof your house in the same manner as if you had a newborn baby. Don't leave anything out that your puppy could perceive as a chew toy. The chances that your puppy will chew your most expensive piece of furniture or an electrical cord are high. It has no idea what is valuable or dangerous. If you cannot supervise your puppy, you should crate or isolate it. Get the puppy tired so it sleeps more during this stage and doesn't get into trouble.

Also, during teething, have toys ready for your puppy to chew to relieve its itching, anxiety and irritability. Choose toys that absorb pressure, such as rubber toys and wooden sticks. Ice cubes work well to numb and cool the gums. Be careful what you choose for your dog to teethe on because you will teach the dog that the material you allow it to chew now will be fair game later. Wood sticks could be mistaken for furniture. Old shoes could be mistaken for new expensive shoes, and old socks could be mistaken for clothes. In cases in which the dog is biting a lot, try giving it any teething numbing cream.

How to discipline a biting puppy or dog:

Touching certain places on a dog, such as the head and face, will immediately initiate play biting. Running at the dog and stopping in front of it will make the dog run and chase you, creating excitement that can easily turn into biting. Your main goal is to prevent biting before it gets started. You do this by playing games with your dog that don't require tugging or biting, such as retrieving, swimming after a toy or pulling a sled. The genetic purpose for the dog's breed will determine how much it uses its mouth. Sporting dogs use their mouths to retrieve. Terriers kill vermin by biting them. Herding dogs use their mouths to control their animal flocks.

I recommend two ways to discipline a dog for biting: 1) grabbing the scruff (the skin just behind the neck) and 2) pinching the nose.

Scruff correction. While the puppy or dog is biting you, grasp the scruff and shake the dog, at the same time saying, "No bite," in a low, firm voice. If you have done this correctly, the second time your dog attempts to bite you, say, "No bite," first and then give the scruff correction. Remember, it's normal for a puppy, or untrained mature dog, to interact with others through biting. It will be difficult for your dog to remember not to bite you, so be prepared to give this correction more than once. Try to keep the dog next to you and begin touching and petting its body, avoiding its head. This teaches the dog that a human can touch it, but it can't bite the human who's touching it. If the dog starts to bite again, then discipline it again and go back to touching and petting its body. Do this several times and then go right into a favorite game, such as throwing a ball, thus redirecting its instinct and energy.

Pinching the nose. While the puppy is biting you, reach in and pinch its nose. Make sure you get the whole nose between your fingers. At the same time, say, "No bite," in a low, firm voice. If you have done this correctly, the second time your dog attempts to bite you, first say, "No bite," and then give the correction. Again, it's normal for your puppy to interact with you through biting, so it will have trouble remembering not to bite. This means you will have to repeat the correction more than once. As with the scruff correction, keep the puppy near you, touching and petting its body. If it starts to bite, repeat the correction and go back to touching and petting it. Do this several times and then go into a favorite game as described above.

If biting and chewing become extreme, you can use a cone collar to help correct the behavior. For how and when to use the cone collar, see the chapter for "Veterinarians."

Un-neutered male dogs:

At the first indication of a female in heat, the male dog's behavior becomes directly challenging if faced by another dog or human. The dog will want to fight off other males and may transfer that desire to humans if the dog perceives you as an obstacle between it and the female. When it is thinking about procreation, the male dog's mating instinct can surface in a split second. Its sex drive can be so strong that it may be unable to eat or think about anything else, thus becoming irritable and much more prone to relieve its feelings by biting. Un-neutered male dogs are more likely to bite than neutered dogs.[6]

Safety tips for current and future dog owners:

☐ Don't let your dog roam free; the dog will think the whole area belongs to it and will protect it.

☐ Before getting a dog, do some research on the breed.

☐ Socialize your dog around people and other dogs.

☐ Train your dog to respect common commands.

☐ Keep your dog healthy.

☐ Spay or neuter your dog.

☐ Don't play rough games or wrestle with your dog.

☐ Have everyone in the family train the dog — even the kids.

☐ Don't chain or tie your dog up.

☐ Get to know what makes your dog afraid and what makes it happy.

Five easy ways to manage your dog's relationship with your children:

☐ Never leave a dog alone with children. The dog may respect the adults, but if adults leave, the dog may think it's the leader and will bite to convey that to the child.

---

[6] CDC website: *www.cdc.gov/mmwr/preview/mmwrhtml/00047723.htm.*

☐ Make sure your dog is socialized with children so it doesn't mistake your child's behavior as threatening or think it is prey.

☐ Be aware that children don't understand the dog's warning signs, thus making them vulnerable to being bitten.

☐ Don't let children hug and kiss the dog. Dogs don't communicate affection in the same manner as we do.

☐ Dogs with a high prey drive and killing instinct have a higher risk for biting children. See the final chapter, "Dogs That Are Dangerous or Fighters, Because of Breeding or Learned Behavior."

What your children should understand about approaching service dogs:

A service dog assists a person with a disability. These dogs have specific tasks and should not be disturbed at any time. They are not dangerous to others, but the attentions of others, especially children who don't know any better, can be dangerous to the dog's owner. A service dog is working even when it appears to be resting. Its disabled owner/handler depends on the dog, and any contact with it could distract the dog from its job of assisting him. The service dog has had many hours of training before a disabled person receives it. After that, day-to-day training modifies the dog's training to fit the disabled person's needs. So the next time you see a service dog, control your children's impulse to pet it, and educate your children about how important the dog is to its disabled owner.

Preventing bites by teaching your dog to wear a muzzle:

As a responsible dog owner, you should train your dog to wear a muzzle because it can prevent bites from occurring. Sometimes circumstances may require your dog to be muzzled, as at the veterinarian's, the groomer's or in large crowded areas. A muzzle makes the dog feel vulnerable because it removes the dog's only way of protecting itself. If your dog is not trained to wear a muzzle, it may view the muzzle as a kind of stress, which could lead to aggression.

Most muzzles I have seen used are fitted too tightly around the dog's mouth, which may make the dog believe it is being disciplined. One form of dog-to-dog discipline is one dog taking the other to the ground. The dog giving the discipline may hold the other dog down by placing his mouth over the other's muzzle, resulting in the disciplined dog being unable to open its mouth. This requires the pinned down dog to breathe through its nose, something the dog is not accustomed to. A too tight muzzle that forces the dog to breathe only through its nose will make it feel disciplined and may cause it to panic and become unpredictable — possibly dangerous.

A few types of muzzles from which to choose include: wire basket, leather basket, leather woven, soft padded and nylon or mesh muzzles. My favorite is the wire basket. This type of muzzle prevents bites while still allowing your dog to breathe freely.

1. Getting started. First, choose a muzzle that allows the dog to open and close its mouth freely. This will enable it to breathe normally. Don't make the first experience with a muzzle uncomfortable or painful. You don't want to make a strong negative imprint, making the progression to liking, or at least accepting, the muzzle slower.

2. Proper fit. Muzzles come in different sizes, so make sure you purchase one that is right for your dog. Look at the breed size chart to assist you in choosing the right size. Most pet stores will allow your dog to enter the store, so try on different sizes until you find the one that fits your dog the best. Muzzles have straps or clips that attach behind the ears. In order to know if the muzzle is tight enough you should be able to pull the muzzle forward and/or lift gently up from the dog's head without the muzzle coming off. If you choose a basket type muzzle, the dog's nose should just be touching the end of the muzzle, but not pressing up against it.

3. The two stages of muzzle training. Having your dog obedience trained will help make the new muzzle experience easier. You have to go through two stages of training to make your dog feel confident and comfortable wearing the muzzle: a) acclimating the dog to the muzzle and b) getting the dog to like the muzzle under stressful conditions.

a. Acclimating the dog to the muzzle. Train the dog so that having something over its mouth is a game. You can do this by placing a reward inside the muzzle, making the dog reach in to take the reward. Do this as many times as it takes until your dog sees the muzzle, thinks reward and places its mouth in without hesitation. The reward could be anything the dog likes, treats or toys. Reserve all other forms of reward-giving and play until the dog learns this step.

Next, hold the muzzle on the dog without strapping it on. Hold it for about two seconds; then remove it and give a reward. Gradually extend the time, holding it until you've reached about ten seconds. If needed, give the "sit-stay" command while holding the muzzle in place.

After the dog has allowed the muzzle to be held in place for ten seconds, strap it on, making sure it is not tight at first. Leave the muzzle on for five seconds and then take it off and reward. Gradually work your way up to strapping it on tightly. If at any time the dog attempts to remove the muzzle by pawing or dropping its head, *do not* correct or say "no." This will only add stress and make the dog try harder to remove the muzzle. If this occurs, either go back to the reward in the muzzle or attach a leash to the dog to keep the dog's head up. Make the sessions short and reward lavishly after each session.

b. Testing the dog under stress. A test under stress occurs whenever the dog feels that it has to use its mouth and the muzzle prevents it from doing so. Before testing the dog under stress, you should make it perform obedience exercises with the muzzle on. This will signal to the dog that you are in control when the muzzle is on and that you will not allow the dog to remove the muzzle at any time. While doing obedience avoid long straight walks. Keep moving at a normal to fast pace. Fast walking and frequent turns will force the dog to move its feet and not allow it to think about the muzzle.

If at any time the dog attempts to remove or paw at the muzzle, do not correct it. Simply make a directional change (right or left turn, circle right or left, u-turn), forcing its front legs to pivot. When the dog is walking comfortably, remove the muzzle and reward the dog. If the dog views the sessions as stressful by walking behind you slowly with its head down and ears back, but obeys you anyway, make sure you give the dog an outlet for its stress after removing the muzzle. You can do this by playing games with it such as retrieving, swimming, etc. You will know you have conquered the muzzle when the dog shows it is comfortable with it by walking at a normal pace, obeying your commands, not attempting to remove the muzzle and holding its head up.

Helping your dog serve its purpose in life:

The dog has two purposes: serving you through obedience and satisfying its own instincts. Proper training helps the dog control its impulses. Training creates standards of behavior to fit your life style and makes your expectations for good behavior valid.

Based on your dog's genetic makeup, its instinct may tell it to guard, herd, dig holes, pull or track. If your life style conflicts with the dog's instincts, you can often channel them into kinds of play that release their energy. These could include playing Frisbee, fetching balls or swimming.

In finding your dog's purpose in life, you need to balance your show of affection and create a bond through play. Too much affection will make the dog emotionally confused about its true purpose in life.

How dogs bond with us:

Dogs bond with humans through long positive contact, through teamwork and through their dependence on us for food. Proper obedience training can account for the majority of the long positive contact. Teamwork in the wild is created through hunting. Domestic dogs experience teamwork with humans when they serve us by performing the instinctual purpose associated with their particular breed. By releasing the dog's instincts through play or work you replace the bond that would have otherwise been created through hunting. In the wild, the feeding ritual which takes place after the hunt is transformed for the domesticated dog into the owner's placing the dog's food in the bowl, resulting in the dog's dependence on the owner for its survival.

Dog-to-dog rough play. Through playing and pretend fighting with each other, puppies and grown dogs learn their individual strengths and weaknesses. Such play teaches them how to protect themselves against other dogs or dangers and prepares them to become leaders in their pack. When you see two dogs playing, notice how they will aim for each other's face and neck. This play fighting is a lot like a real dog fight, except that in a dog fight either dog may get badly hurt. To avoid such problems have your dog play with other dogs that have a similar temperament.

Dog-to-human rough play. The more you let any dog use its teeth on you, or on other dogs, the stronger and more aggressive the dog may become toward you or other dogs. A play bite may be just as painful as an aggressive bite. Because children have fragile skin, it doesn't take much force to cause injury.

If a dog bites your child in play and you have to go to the doctor, he may not understand that the bite was only in fun. The doctor will have to notify Animal Control or the local police. Either one may insist that the dog be taken away or even destroyed.

Rough play with dogs can:

- ☐ cause the dog to begin viewing your hands as the human version of its own mouth and teeth and target them for biting

- ☐ promote threatening behavior because the dog plays to figure out who is the boss

- ☐ result in an accidental scratch which others might consider to be a bite and take more seriously than is warranted

- ☐ get the dog too excited, so the play turns into serious biting

- ☐ encourage the dog to start treating humans like dogs and challenge new people it meets

- ☐ encourage the dog to use its teeth on people, biting harder as it gets older

- ☐ make the dog possessive, especially if playing the chasing game with a toy. The dog will think the toy belongs to it and will defend it with a bite if you try to take it away, even if it knows you well. If you and your children play fetch with a dog, wear gloves to avoid accidental bites on your hands. Also, be aware that the dog may accidentally bite other parts of your body while trying to get its toy.

For a discussion of how rough play will make certain dogs very dangerous, see the chapter on "Dogs That Are Dangerous or Fighters, Because of Breeding or Learned Behavior."

Dogs' behavior when kids are playing:

When kids play, they become animated running back and forth, screaming, falling down, getting up, then running again. This behavior may get the dog excited and want to join in. When it does, its teeth and mouth become the equivalents of our hands. As the dog runs, it jumps at the kids, grabbing with its mouth and biting. These play-bites can become serious if the dog gets momentum while running or decides to bite down and the kids pull away at the same time. Keep the dog secure while kids are playing until you have observed its temperament and reactions to the kids' excited playing. This will give you an idea of what the dog may or may not do when kids are playing.

Petting:

Some dogs may associate a person's reaching out to pet them with pain, especially if they have been mistreated or trained using forceful methods. If a negative feeling surfaces or if the dog perceives reaching for it as a threat, it may bite. All dogs have a personal space, averaging about zero to six feet. Even if it's your own dog, you should respect that space. Because dogs can't talk, they may growl and then bite or just bite to tell you to leave them alone.

Startled dog:

Through no fault of its own, if you startle or hurt a dog by stepping on it or tripping over it, even your own dog may bite you out of its pain or fear reflex. Make sure you make a noise prior to walking over a dog or going by it.

Reasons why you shouldn't treat your dog like a human:

The dog's instinct is to be your servant. This is a very hard thing for some people to understand. If left in the wild, no dog would serve only as an emotional support for other dogs. All dogs would have to play their instinctual parts in the pack.

Domestication has not altered this instinct. Your dog depends on you for food and shelter; therefore, it will rely on you for pack leadership. When you treat your dog like a human, you create frustration and confusion, because such treatment goes against the dog's natural instinct. Your dog naturally wants to act and be treated like a dog, not a human. If you treat your dog like a human, it will treat you like a dog.

Conflicting dog expressions:

These are conflicting signals that have been misinterpreted as aggressiveness. Wrongly interpreted, they have cost innocent dogs their homes and sometimes their lives. Knowing these conflicting signals will give you the added edge on saving the life of your dog or of someone else's. Here is how you can tell the difference.

1. Smiling versus snarling. For humans, a smile is a facial expression shown by turning up the corners of the mouth. For dogs, it is a squeeze upward of their nose and muzzle, with the skin drawn back exposing their teeth. However, this is very similar to a snarl. A dog baring its teeth can be very intimidating, so recognizing how to differentiate between snarl-

Snarling

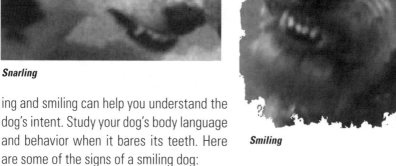

Smiling

ing and smiling can help you understand the dog's intent. Study your dog's body language and behavior when it bares its teeth. Here are some of the signs of a smiling dog:

- ☐ It is showing its teeth when it greets you.
- ☐ It is moving in a relaxed way. If it is snarling the dog's body will be stiff.
- ☐ Its head is moving freely.
- ☐ It looks excited but not angry (eyes soft not glaring).
- ☐ It usually doesn't make any noise. If it is snarling, it will also probably be giving a low growl.

2. Grumbling versus growling. Grumbling is a pleasurable noise that usually occurs when you are massaging or scratching your dog or when it gets very excited. Grumbling is often confused with a growl. The difference is that the feeling good noise comes when the dog's body and face are relaxed. Growling is accompanied by a frozen, tensed body and face.

3. Snapping or clenching teeth. Some dogs do this when playing or when they have it in mind to bite. The noise from the teeth hitting together sounds intimidating even in play. When playing, the dog may miss biting the toy, causing its teeth to snap together. The dog's excitement may also cause it to snap its teeth involuntarily, as a way of showing excitement.

On the other hand, some dogs will snap their teeth together in anticipation of biting. This is especially true of dogs in training for police work. The dog gets so frustrated during protection training that its teeth will hit together when anticipating a bite.

Knowing your dog's habits and body language will assist you in determining if the snapping is a threat or just a way of communicating excitement during play. If you have a dog that was trained in protection, you need to be especially aware of what its snapping may mean.

How to understand a dog's body language:

Study the body language of dogs in your day-to-day interactions with them. What makes a dog excited? What makes it fearful? What stresses it? How does your behavior contribute to the dog's behavior? Familiarize yourself with other types of dogs with different temperaments and from different breeds. Notice especially *how* the different kinds of dogs look when they are experiencing various emotions ranging from excitement and joy to fear and aggressiveness. Before long, you will begin anticipating your dog's behaviors just by the way it looks, and you will be able to do this for the other types of dogs you have studied.

The dog's eyes are very hard to read. Because they are small, you have to get close up to study them. When the dog is afraid or ready to attack, its eyes glare, even if it is excited about biting you. When the dog is happy or excited in a friendly way, its eyes look soft. When the dog is sick or sad, its eyes look weak.

Below are the most common body language signs associated with the behaviors you need to know about. Once these become recognizable, you should begin to expand your knowledge by learning the mixed signals dogs give because of undesirable genetics, incorrect training and poor environment. Also, dogs' body language varies according to whether or not they have a tail or have prick or floppy ears.

Remember that the dog's body language does not lie. It does not use its body language to trap you into getting bitten. Dogs may be master manipulators when they want their way, but, to our advantage, they do not use manipulation when they intend to attack or bite.

1. Friendly or playful body language:

- [ ] Total body is moving side to side while moving forward in a relaxed way.
- [ ] Face is relaxed while moving.
- [ ] Mouth is opening and closing, relaxed.
- [ ] Dog is bouncing off the ground with its body swinging.
- [ ] Front legs are stretched out forward with rear end in the air so that the dog appears to be bowing with its whole body wiggling.
- [ ] Dog is moving forward then stopping, while bouncing from side to side.

Friendly

2. Potentially threatening body language:

- [ ] Dog's head is turned but it is still looking at you.
- [ ] Dog is circling you, attempting to attack from behind. *Good time to utilize dog repellent spray or high-pitched sound devices.*
- [ ] Head is carried high or low—high head shows a dominant dog; low head shows a fearful dog.

☐ Dog is looking back and forth quickly, while retreating (shows a nervous or fearful dog).

☐ Could be barking or silent; it does not matter which.

☐ Mouth is tensed when closed with lips pulled back tight — could be growling.

☐ Front legs are stretched out forward with rear end in the air so that the dog appears to be bowing, *but its body is stiff, not moving.*

Potentially threatening

3. Dangerous body language:

☐ A surge of adrenaline will surface, and the dog's body will stiffen. The stiffness will happen whether the dog is moving or still.

☐ Hackles (hair along the neck and spine) will rise.

☐ Teeth could be showing. Dogs with large muzzle skin will seldom show teeth because they are unable to lift the muzzle skin.

☐ Dog maintains direct eye contact that results in tunnel vision. The dog doesn't get distracted by any other movement around it and is unable to hear its owner's commands.

Dangerous

☐ Dog is barking and not moving, trying to warn you to stay away.

☐ The dog's tail could be wagging because it is happy and excited about biting you. A dog with its tail tucked under may bite you out of fear.

☐ The dog makes a fast, direct approach then stops; its next approach may be to bite you. *Good time to utilize dog repellent spray or high-pitched sound devices.*

KIDS

How to Prepare for Dog Encounters and Prevent Bites

Any dog can be a threat. All dogs will bite when protecting themselves, their property, and/or their owners. Since dogs can't talk, they will bite to tell you "No" or "Stop" — even if it's your own dog.

How can you tell the difference between a dog encounter and an attack? In a dog encounter, the dog will confront you but decide not to attack. In an attack the dog has decided to bite you. It's hard to tell when a dog encounter will turn into an attack. Sometimes you surprise a dog and it will attack right away, or it may first try to warn you off. You can't know what any dog will do in the face of stress, so you have to be prepared for both a harmless encounter and an actual attack when you meet a dog. You don't want to injure or kill a harmless dog, but you don't want to get bitten either. The detailed instructions and checklists that follow will help you know what is best to do in a simple encounter and an outright attack.

Twelve safety precautions for avoiding getting bitten:

- [ ] Never run from any dog — running triggers the dog's hunting instinct. The dog may not have been planning to bite you, but if you run the dog now thinks it should bite.

- [ ] Never scream at a dog or scream while playing. To the dog, screaming signals distress and vulnerability. If you scream, the dog may think you are a kind of prey that is in distress and thus vulnerable to attack, or your screaming may frighten the dog, which could then bite you out of fear.

- [ ] Never turn your back on any dog. The dog may already be afraid. If you turn away or run, the dog's instinct will tell it to chase you and bite you out of its own fear. Such a dog is a fear biter.

- [ ] Never assume some dogs are friendly — just because it's friendly to one person does not mean it will be friendly towards you.

- [ ] Don't trust your friend's or a stranger's opinion of her dog. The average person thinks her dog will not bite. Don't approach or pet an unfamiliar dog. You wouldn't start talking to and touching a human stranger; the same goes for dogs.

- [ ] Don't kiss or hug your own or anybody else's dog. Dogs don't show affection with a kiss, as we do. A hug invades the dog's space and challenges it, and it may bite to tell you to stop.

- [ ] Leave dogs alone when they're eating, sleeping, or caring for puppies.

- [ ] Never hit or kick a dog.

- [ ] If dog is tied up, stay away. If you enter its space, it may bite.

- [ ] Never pet a dog over a fence.

- [ ] Leave a dog alone if it's injured. Pain will make it bite to tell you to leave it alone.

- [ ] Never try to lift a dog by the front end. Putting your hands under the dog's front legs (armpits) causes pain.

If at a friend's house:

Not every dog is your friend and should be trusted. You may think your dog will like your friends the same way it likes you, and you may think your friends' dogs will like you the way they like them. You may think that you can pet and play with an unfamiliar dog the same way you do with dogs you know well. Unfortunately, this is not true. A family dog has no commitment to kids outside its family pack. The dog doesn't know these outside kids are its owner's friends or relatives. You must learn that you won't necessarily be able to interact with your friends' dogs the same way your friends interact with their dogs.

Before you can pet and play with your friends' dogs, they have to get to know you in a controlled situation, in which the dog is under obedience commands such as "sit," "down" and "stay." Only time will make your friends' dogs learn to trust you as they do their family members. When you visit a friend who has a dog you don't know well, follow these precautions:

- ☐ Ask politely for them to put the dog away until the dog gets to know you.

- ☐ Don't think because the dog likes your friend it will like you.

- ☐ Wait to get to know the dog before playing with it or petting it. An older dog will not want to be bothered and may have its own rules on how to be treated.

- ☐ Begin petting or playing with the dog when it is under obedience controls.

- ☐ Don't pet and play with the dog when it is not under obedience controls until you are *sure* the dog accepts you.

Eleven safety tips for dog encounters:

- ☐ Do not run; you will only cause the dog's biting instinct to surface.

- ☐ If a dog is following you; stop and evaluate the situation. The dog may just want to smell you.

- ☐ Stop stand sideways, so the dog doesn't think you're challenging it.

- ☐ Avoid quick movement. The dog could be nervous, and a quick movement may trigger its fear-biting impulse.

- ☐ Give common commands ("stay," "sit," "down"). If you know the dog's name, relax it by using its name. Be careful giving negative commands ("no," "get out of here"). Negative commands may work, but if a dog perceives them as a threat, it may bite you.

- ☐ If the dog is coming towards you, move backwards and sideways, keeping your eye on the dog. This gives you space and time to react.

- ☐ Look at the dog, but don't stare into its eyes. Look at the top of the dog's head or eyebrows. Looking away may tell the dog it has won the challenge, and it may bite you.

- ☐ Once the dog loses interest in you, move slowly backwards until it is out of sight.

- ☐ Provide the dog room for an escape by not cutting off escape routes such as a door or gate.

- ☐ Remain calm and confident by taking deep breaths. This will calm your body. Dogs can sense tension and fear. If the dog senses your fear (and it probably will), it will gain the confidence to bite you.

- ☐ If cornered, wait until dog loses interest in you.

Defending yourself against a dog attack: stop, drop and curl:

If the attack is imminent, fall to the ground and curl up in a ball, protecting your stomach, face and ears. Do not scream or yell, this will only make the dog more confident. Its survival instinct will surface, and it will attack you with renewed force. Once on the ground, you are no longer a threat. Listen to what the dog is doing. Try to keep an eye on the dog while standing up slowly.

How to defend yourself if an attack is threatened but not imminent:

- ☐ Stop and stand sideways, so the dog doesn't think you're challenging it.
- ☐ Be aware of what the dog is doing at all times.
- ☐ As the dog is running towards you, walk backwards and sideways.
- ☐ Wave a shirt, hat or sack to present a moving target to distract and confuse the dog.
- ☐ Depending on what you have near you, (chair, bike, skateboard) pick up any object and hold it in front of you.
- ☐ Don't try to hit the dog.
- ☐ If you have nothing to hold in front of you, get behind a tree, fence or car keeping your back against the object.
- ☐ Climb backwards on top of any object (car, fence, tree).
- ☐ If you fall or are knocked down, curl into a ball and protect your stomach, face and ears with anything you have.
- ☐ Stand up moving slowly.

Loose dogs and stray dogs:

A loose dog has been allowed to determine its own territory, and it now believes that area belongs to it. It will protect the area against anyone who comes into it. If a loose or stray dog scares you, notify Animal Control or the police.

Rough play:

Through playing and pretend fighting with each other, puppies and grown dogs learn their individual strengths and weaknesses. Such play teaches them how to protect themselves against other dogs or dangers and prepares them to become leaders in their pack. When you see two dogs playing, notice how they will aim for each other's face and neck. This play fighting is a lot like a real dog fight, except that in a dog fight either dog may get badly hurt.

When you rough play with a dog, however, you could get into a serious problem. The dog will play fight with you as if you were another dog, but its biting will hurt you a lot more than it would hurt another dog. Your body isn't protected with a thick fur coat or loose skin that is hard to hold onto. Your unprotected skin is tender and easy to keep hold of. If a dog bites you in play and you have to go to the doctor or hospital, the people there may not understand that the bite was only in fun. If the bite is bad enough, they may insist that the dog be taken away or even killed. Here are the problems created by rough playing with dogs:

- ☐ It promotes threatening behavior because the dog plays to figure out who is the boss.
- ☐ It leads to jumping on you and others.
- ☐ The dog gets too excited and may knock you down and hurt you.
- ☐ What started as play turns into serious biting.
- ☐ The dog starts treating humans like dogs and challenges new people it meets.
- ☐ It encourages the dog to use its teeth on people, and as it gets older it may bite harder.
- ☐ It makes the dog possessive, especially if playing the chasing game with a toy. The dog will think it owns the toy and will defend it. Even if the dog knows you well, it may bite you for trying to take the toy away.
- ☐ If you play fetch with a dog, wear a glove to avoid accidental bites on your hand, but be cautious because the dog may accidentally bite other parts of your body.

For a discussion of how rough play will make certain dogs very dangerous, see the chapter on "Dogs That Are Dangerous or Fighters, Because of Breeding or Learned Behavior."

Kids get bitten in the face because humans and dogs interpret affection differently:

When I was a kid, I believed that all dogs were friendly. If I saw a dog acting friendly toward someone else, I assumed it would be friendly towards me. I assumed that my affection would be accepted; after all, it was a good thing the dog was getting. I was shown otherwise by a dog that bit me in the face. Kids get so excited at seeing a puppy or dog that they don't think about being afraid of any aggressive behavior the dog may show. But, just as kids are cautious about showing affection towards strangers, they should be equally cautious about showing affection towards other people's dogs and stray dogs.

Human kisses versus dog "kisses":

A kiss brings people emotionally closer. We try to transfer that to our dogs. We believe the dog is kissing us when we place our faces close to their faces to kiss it and receive a lick from the dog. When we talk in a high-pitched voice and stroke or massage a dog while kissing or nuzzling it, the dog has been conditioned to get excited and will begin to lick us, just as they lick each other when they get excited. Humans think this is a kiss, but it isn't.

In most cases, the dog you have a long-term bond with will accept or tolerate your kiss, but dogs you have no close connection with may interpret your kiss as an invasion of their personal space or a way of initiating play. Because dogs are territorial, they resent having their personal space invaded. I use this to my advantage when training police dogs in protection. I invade the dog's space to elicit a bite. How close you have to get to do this varies from dog to dog.

When a kid approaches a dog that is lying down or in a cage or kennel, the dog will feel confined or even cornered, so it will be more protective of its space than if it were standing up or out in the open. Unfortunately, kids tend to kiss dogs when they are lying down because they feel more cuddly toward them in this position. When you put your face too close and a dog feels threatened, it will probably bite the closest thing to it — your face. If the dog thinks you are inviting it to play, it will also probably bite your face, because when dogs play with each other they target the other dog's face and neck.

A dog's teeth are sharp and kids' skin is fragile, so it's easy for a dog to cause injury if a tooth only grazes a kid's face in play. If the dog bites out of aggression, the bite will be much worse and can happen in seconds. The dog responds so quickly, almost involuntarily, to having its space invaded that it may not make any warning noise (such as a growl) before it bites. Because kids think that dogs will understand that kissing and hugging show affection, they get bitten on the face a lot.

Also, a lick from a dog is usually unsanitary. One way dogs communicate with each other is through tasting and smelling. They don't find urine and feces disgusting, as we do. Other dogs' excrement gives them useful information, so it's normal for them to smell each others' backsides. Smelling or tasting a female's urine can tell a male dog if the female is in heat and ready for breeding. Allowing dogs to lick your face, when it may have just used that mouth on another dog's private parts, is unhealthy and may contribute to passing some diseases from the dog to you.

So what does a lick from a dog mean? Dogs lick to groom each other the way they groom themselves, to show submission, to give a respectful greeting or to stimulate another dog's mouth to get regurgitated food to eat. Female dogs will lick their pups to stimulate them to move and to keep them clean. If a dog smells something on your skin that it likes, it will lick you, especially after you have eaten or have had a sweaty workout. This is not a kiss. A dog's nature does not allow it to show affection by licking (or what you might call "kissing").

How dogs view human hugs:

A human hug conveys an affectionate personal connection or greeting. A hug to a dog is the complete opposite. It conveys a challenge for dominance. A quick hug of the dog's neck will either startle it into biting you or tell the dog you are challenging it. A dog connects pressure on its neck to challenges or a form of discipline through dog body language. This is how dogs communicate with each other. So your dog may interpret the neck pressure exerted by a hug as a challenge or a punishment.

In most cases, the dog you have a long-term bond with will accept or tolerate a hug, as it does your kisses. It knows you are the leader and will not challenge you. But the dog may also see a kid's small stature as showing vulnerability and will know the kid isn't its leader. Such a dog may tolerate a kid's challenge to its space while the adult leader is present, but not when the leader is gone, even for a few seconds. So, the kid's mom leaves the room. The kid continues to hug the dog, and the dog tries to spin or wriggle out of the hug. If it can't escape it may bite the kid so he will release his grip. And in most cases, the kid's face is the closest thing to the dog's mouth. Again, the dog's instinct to escape may make it respond so quickly that it doesn't have time to give a warning growl before it bites.

Dogs put a lot of value on their personal space. If you hold or squeeze them, they may think you are challenging that space and may bite because they can't tell you to let go. While you are hugging the dog, you won't be able to see its warning signs, so you may get bitten when you aren't expecting a problem.

Dogs show their affection, not through "hugs" and "kisses," but by serving us in ways that come naturally to their particular breed. Hunting dogs will bring us trophies of dead animals; digging dogs will excavate their prey for us wherever they find it; water dogs will swim after sticks for us; retrievers will bring back everything we throw for them.

How to understand a dog's body language:

Study the dog's body language while interacting with it. What makes the dog excited? What makes it fearful? What stresses it? What does your behavior contribute to the dog's behavior? Familiarize yourself with various types of dogs with different temperaments and from different breeds. Notice especially *how* the different kinds of dogs look when they are experiencing various emotions ranging from excitement and joy to fear and aggressiveness. Before long you will begin anticipating your dog's behaviors just by the way it looks, and you will be able to do this for the other types of dogs you have studied.

The dog's eyes are very hard to read. Because they are small, you have to get close up to study them. When the dog is afraid or ready to attack, its eyes glare, even if it is excited about biting you. When the dog is happy or excited in a friendly way, its eyes look soft. When the dog is sick or sad, its eyes look weak.

Below are the most common body language signs associated with the behaviors you need to know about. Once these become recognizable, you should begin to expand your knowledge by learning the mixed signals dogs give because of undesirable genetics, incorrect training and poor environment. Also, dogs' body language varies according to whether or not they have a tail or have stand-up or floppy ears.

Remember that the dog's body language does not lie. It does not use its body language to trap you into getting bitten. Dogs may be master manipulators when they want their way, but, to our advantage, they do not use manipulation when they intend to attack or bite.

1. Friendly or playful body language:

☐ Total body is moving side to side while moving forward in a relaxed way.

☐ Face is relaxed while moving.

☐ Mouth is opening and closing, relaxed.

☐ Dog is bouncing off the ground with its body swinging.

Friendly

☐ Front legs are stretched out forward with rear end in the air so that the dog appears to be bowing with its whole body wiggling.

☐ Dog is moving forward then stopping, while bouncing from side to side.

2. Potentially threatening body language:

☐ Dog's head is turned but it is still looking at you.

☐ Dog is circling you, attempting to attack from behind.

☐ Head is carried high or low — high head shows a dominant dog; low head shows a fearful dog.

☐ Dog is looking back and forth quickly, while retreating (shows a nervous or fearful dog).

☐ Could be barking or silent; it does not matter which.

☐ Mouth is tensed when closed with lips pulled back tight — could be growling.

Potentially threatening

☐ Front legs are stretched out forward with rear end in the air so that the dog appears to be bowing, *but its body is stiff, not moving.*

3. Dangerous body language:

☐ A surge of adrenaline will surface, and the dog's body will stiffen. The stiffness will happen whether the dog is moving or still.

☐ Hackles (hair along the neck and spine) will rise.

☐ Teeth could be showing. Dogs with large muzzle skin will seldom show teeth because they are unable to lift the muzzle skin.

Dangerous

☐ Dog maintains direct eye contact that results in tunnel vision. The dog doesn't get distracted by any other movement around it and is unable to hear its owner's commands.

☐ Dog is barking and not moving, trying to warn you to stay away.

☐ The dog's tail could be wagging because it is happy and excited about biting you. A dog with its tail tucked under may bite you out of fear.

☐ The dog makes a fast, direct approach then stops; its next approach may be to bite you.

Keep in mind:

If the attack is imminent and you are knocked down to the ground, curl up in a protective ball. It is not instinctive for a single, domesticated dog, or dogs without a strong killing instinct, to attack its prey when its prey is motionless. This is the same concept that you may have learned about bear attacks. Usually, neither a bear nor a dog will attack a motionless person or prey. This does not hold true for dogs with a strong killing instinct, however. For a description of how they behave, see the chapter on "Dogs That Are Dangerous or Fighters, Because of Breeding or Learned Behavior."

PREPARING YOURSELF
FOR DOG ENCOUNTERS FOR:

RUNNERS, JOGGERS, SKATERS AND WALKERS

Any dog can be a threat. All dogs will bite when protecting themselves, their property, and/or their owners. Since dogs can't talk, they will bite to tell you "No" or "Stop" — even if it's your own dog.

Photo of Traci Ruiz and Apollo

How can you tell the difference between a dog encounter and an attack? In a dog encounter, the dog will confront you but decide not to attack. In an attack the dog has decided to bite you. It's hard to tell when a dog encounter will turn into an attack. Sometimes you surprise a dog and it will attack right away, or it may first try to warn you off. You can't know what any dog will do in the face of stress, so you have to be prepared for both a harmless encounter and an actual attack when you meet a dog. You don't want to injure or kill a harmless dog, but you don't want to get bitten either.

To be sure you can hear the signs of a dog threat, avoid wearing any device over your ears that could muffle sounds. If you run wearing a Walkman, turn it down low enough so you can hear other sounds. The detailed instructions and checklists that follow will help you know what is best to do in a simple encounter and an outright attack.

Five dog encounter survival tips:

- ☐ Never assume all dogs are friendly. A dog's behavior can change suddenly and without any warning. Dogs under stress are unpredictable, and even cute dogs will bite.
- ☐ Never run from any dog — running triggers the dog's hunting instinct and makes it chase you.
- ☐ Stop, then turn and walk slowly backwards keeping an eye on the dog. This will also prepare you to strike the dog if it attacks.
- ☐ Never turn your back on any dog. The dog may already be afraid. If you turn away or run, the dog's instinct will tell it to chase you and bite you out of its own fear. Such a dog is a fear-biter. Also, if you run away, you will not be able to watch the dog's body language, and it may bite while you're not looking.
- ☐ Don't stand face to face during a threat from a dog. This will only challenge the dog to a fight.

When passing by an area, check for:

- ☐ "Beware of Dog" signs
- ☐ dog house, chains, bowls
- ☐ dog feces in the yard — the smell may strike you before you actually see them
- ☐ patches of dead grass where the dog's urine has killed it
- ☐ worn track around fence — this indicates that the dog is out a lot.
- ☐ If passing by an area you know has a dog, make some noise while approaching the property.
- ☐ If the dog is in a yard where an underground electric fence is confining it, don't consider that type of fence a valid means of containment. The dog may get a rush of adrenaline and cross the fence line. The dog's state of aggression will numb its body from the shock and it may bite you.

Defending yourself during a dog encounter:

☐ Avoid quick movement. The dog could be nervous. A quick movement may trigger fear, and it may bite out of fear.

☐ If a dog is following you, stop and evaluate the situation. Give it some common commands ("stay," "sit," "down"). This makes the dog think maybe you are in charge.

☐ Be careful about giving negative commands ("no," "get out of here"). Negative commands may work, but if a dog perceives them as a threat you may escalate the dog's aggression and get bitten.

☐ If you know the dog, relax it by using its name.

☐ Do not try to outrun the dog. You will only cause its biting instinct to surface.

☐ Stop and stand sideways, so the dog doesn't think you are challenging it.

☐ If the dog is coming towards you, move backwards and sideways, keeping an eye on the dog. This will give you space and time to react.

☐ Look at the dog, but don't stare into its eyes. Look at the top of the dog's head or at its eyebrows. Looking away may tell the dog it has won the challenge, and it may bite you.

☐ Once the dog loses interest in you, move slowly backwards until it is out of sight.

☐ Provide the dog room for an escape by not cutting off escape routes such as a door or gate.

☐ Remain calm by taking deep breaths. This will relax your body. Dogs can sense tension and fear. If the dog senses your fear (and it probably will), it will gain confidence about biting you.

☐ If you are cornered, wait until the dog loses interest in you. This usually takes only a few minutes, so be patient and wait it out. Then move slowly away.

If owner is present:

☐ If the dog is aggressive, keep your eye on it and insist that the owner keep it under control, saying, "You *need* to have your dog under control."

☐ If you take your eyes off the dog, it may think it has won the challenge and bite you.

☐ Insist the dog be under control.

☐ Avoid getting angry.

☐ Do not enter property; stay on road or sidewalk. Entering its owner's property may give the dog no other option but to bite.

- [ ] Warn the owner that, if her dog threatens you again, you will notify Animal Control.
- [ ] Depending on the circumstances, notify Animal Control without a warning.

Defensive tactics during a dog encounter:

- [ ] Carry dog repellent spray. See below for how to use repellent spray.
- [ ] Carry a high-pitched sound device. See below for how to use the device.
- [ ] Carry rocks and, if necessary, throw them sidearm at the dog, so the dog doesn't see your raised arm as a threat.
- [ ] Carry a stick about one foot long, in case you need to strike the dog.
- [ ] Remove tennis shoes, hit them together to make a loud noise. If that doesn't work, throw them at the dog.
- [ ] Stop moving forward and slowly walk backwards, keeping your eye on the dog.

Defending yourself against a dog attack: stop, drop and curl:

If the attack is imminent, fall on the ground and curl up in a ball, protecting your vital organs, face and ears. Do not scream or yell. This will only make the dog more confident. Its survival instinct will surface, and it will attack with renewed force. Once you are on the ground and silent, you are no longer a threat. If an attack isn't imminent:

- [ ] Stop and stand sideways so the dog doesn't think you're challenging it.
- [ ] Remain aware of the dog at all times.
- [ ] Provide an escape for the dog so it doesn't feel cornered.

- [ ] As the dog is running toward you, walk backwards and sideways, so you can keep an eye on the dog, being ready to hit it if you have to.
- [ ] Turning around and walking away while looking over your shoulder at the dog may make it bite you out of fear. Turning your back on the dog also keeps you from making a good solid hit at it if you have to.
- [ ] Wave a shirt, hat or sack to present a moving target and to distract and confuse the dog.

Don't run or turn your back.

☐ If the dog is biting you, use dog repellent spray or strike the dog. See below for how to use repellent spray and striking techniques.

☐ If bitten *don't pull away*. This is very difficult to do, but if you pull away, the bite will be much more serious because the dog will resist having anything pulled from its mouth and will fight harder to hold on, causing more skin-tearing and deeper wounds.

☐ If you fall or are knocked down curl up in a protective ball as outlined at the beginning of this section. Listen to determine if the dog is still in the area. Listen to hear if the dog is still there. If it is but is not sounding threatening, stand up slowly while keeping an eye on the dog.

Roller blade skaters:

A person moving on wheels (such as in-line skates) may excite the dog. This could trigger it to chase you and bite you or make physical contact that could upset your balance and cause a fall. If a dog starts after you, stop on grass or other surface that will give you stability and a soft landing if you do fall. Then follow the steps for defending yourself against a dog encounter or attack.

Skate boarders:

Stop and get off the board. You can use the board to block the dog by putting it in front of you. Then follow the steps for defending yourself against a dog encounter. If the attack is imminent, use the board as a barrier by swinging it from side to side, creating a wall between you and the dog. This will make it difficult for the dog to determine when to attack, thus keeping it away from you.

How to use dog repellent spray:

Whatever brand or type of dog repellent spray you decide to use, read the directions carefully. Check the can regularly to make sure it's still in working order. Do this by shaking the contents vigorously and spraying a small amount. Don't spray too much because repeated testing will use up the spray and leave you with too little when you really need it. If it is cold, make sure the brand you use doesn't freeze. Keep it warm by putting it next to your body.

Dog repellent spray is a nonlethal product that temporarily disorients the dog by surprising it. Dogs don't expect you to reach out and touch them without using your hands. The spray also gives the dog a quick liquid sting and causes temporary eye and nose irritation which distracts it. When it feels the irritation, it will attempt to rub off the substance by pawing at it or rolling on the ground. If you spray the repellent in the dog's mouth, it will immediately begin salivating and be distracted from biting. If the wind is low and the repellent's pressure is at full strength, most sprays can reach up to 12 feet.

In my experience, dog repellent spray works on dogs that have not decided to bite but may do so at any time, such as dogs that are circling you or barking at you but not moving. Don't think the spray is your main line of defense. Dogs that are attacking or are intent on biting you may see it as a threat or a challenge, and in their desire to overcome this challenge will become more aggressive. Such dogs are full of adrenaline and may not feel the effects of the spray.

When using dog repellent spray:

- ☐ Remember that although you have been told to spray the dog's eyes, that is an almost impossible target to hit. Compared to humans' eyes, dogs have much larger tear ducts and a third eyelid. These assist them in recovering faster. I have been more successful spraying the dog in the mouth. This stimulates the dog's licking reflex, thus stopping it from biting. Also, the mouth is a much larger target.

- ☐ If the dog is biting you or has its face very close to you, try spraying into its nostrils. This will instantly cause maximum irritation and the dog will back off.

- ☐ Spray in a figure eight motion, creating a continuous wall of spray. This will give you a greater chance of hitting some part of the dog's face.

- ☐ Start spraying as soon as you see the dog coming at you, assuming you have the can out and are ready to use it. You must be ready, because a delay will allow the dog to get too close to you or actually begin biting you.

- ☐ Walk backwards keeping an eye on the dog. This creates space and gives you time to think about your other options. See below for how to use striking techniques.

- ☐ Give verbal obedience commands to the dog ("sit," "down" or "stay") as you are walking backwards.

- ☐ While walking backwards, you are also escaping. Some dogs think they have done their jobs when you have gone away from their territory.

High-pitched sound devices:

These emit a high-pitched tone that humans can't hear but dogs can. The device should be used as soon as the dog encounter becomes threatening. These devices cause discomfort to the dog's hearing but have no negative aftereffects. They are about the size of a garage-door opener and fit in the palm of your hand or clip onto your waistband or belt. When you push the activating button, the dog first becomes surprised because it can't tell where the high-pitched sound is coming from. Then it quickly realizes that as it gets closer to you, the sound gets more intense. Being surprised and disturbed by the sound, the dog may not come any closer to you. This device doesn't work on all dogs, but it is an effective protection against dogs that have not yet decided to bite you but could do so at any moment.

Fighting back an attack using striking techniques:

During an attack or if an attack is imminent, you may decide to use striking techniques. Your objective is to destroy the dog's confidence by striking it with dramatic, instant, painful strikes and to survive the encounter with the least amount of injury to yourself. If you think you can't strike the dog effectively, don't use this option. The dog may view your ineffective strikes as a challenge, which will make it fight even harder, thus increasing your chance of injury.

*Kick or knee
to the chest*   *Punch back of the
neck where the
shoulders meet*   *Punch downward with
forearm to the spine*   *Uppercut to
the throat*

How to use striking techniques:

☐ Knee or kick the dog in the chest; this will knock the wind out of it.

☐ If possible get the dog's attention by moving something over your head; this will get the dog to focus on the moving target and expose its chest.

☐ Punch, chop or strike the back of the neck where the shoulders meet or aim for the spine. Use any object that will make an impact.

☐ Use your forearm to punch downward on the dog's spine or drive downward with your body weight going to the ground.

☐ Give an upper cut to the throat.

☐ Slam the dog to the ground or up against a wall.

☐ Keep an eye on the dog at all times.

☐ If the dog retreats, walk backwards to an escape route.

What to do if you are bitten:

☐ Seek medical attention immediately.

☐ Report the dog bite to Animal Control or the police department.

☐ Write down a good description of the dog, the circumstances leading to the bite and the dog owner's name and address.

☐ Seek legal advice if appropriate.

Loose dogs and stray dogs (notify Animal Control or the local police):

A loose dog or a stray dog has been allowed to determine its own territory. The dog now believes its roaming area, regardless of the size, belongs to it. This makes the dog unpredictable even if it appears friendly. Anyone invading its territory will make the dog protect it, so stay away from all stray dogs and notify Animal Control or the local police.

Dogs trained for protection:

While in training to protect its owner and her property, the dog has always been allowed to win. Because of this, the dog's confidence has been so strongly built up that it thinks it can overcome anything a human can give out. Be prepared to divert the dog's attention from you to a target object that it can defeat, such as a hat or sack. While it is attacking the object, it will become vulnerable to your repellent spray, striking techniques or stronger measures.

Dogs not trained for protection:

Similar to a dog trained for protection, a dog not specifically trained for protection will still instinctively protect its house or yard as its territory. It believes that it has won all challenges from people invading its space. After all, as you pass by, it barks; you walk or run on.

The treat myth:

If you carry treats to smooth things over with some dogs, the dogs will see people entering their property as a good thing. The problem arises when strangers see a dog running toward them looking for a treat, and they get confused about what the dog intends. The dog is looking for its treat, but a stranger may well think it is about to attack and will hit it, spray it with dog repellent or use even greater force. Your treats have created a painful, even fatal, trap for the dog.

How to understand a dog's body language:

Study the body language of dogs you encounter while out running, skating or walking. If you have a pet dog, study its body language. What makes a dog excited? What makes it fearful? What stresses it? What does your behavior contribute to the dog's behavior? Familiarize yourself with other types of dogs with different temperaments and from different breeds. Notice especially how the different kinds of dogs look when they are experiencing various emotions ranging from excitement and joy to fear and aggressiveness. Before long you will begin anticipating a particular dog's behavior just by the way it looks, and you will be able to do this for the other types of dogs you have studied.

The dog's eyes are very hard to read. Because they are small, you have to get close up to study them. When the dog is afraid or ready to attack, its eyes glare, even if it is excited about biting you. When the dog is happy or excited in a friendly way, its eyes look soft. When the dog is sick or sad, its eyes look weak.

Below are the most common body language signs associated with the behaviors you need to know about. Once these become recognizable, you should begin to expand your knowledge by learning the mixed signals dogs give because of undesirable genetics, incorrect training and poor environment. Also, dogs' body language varies according to whether or not they have a tail or have prick or floppy ears.

Remember that the dog's body language does not lie. It does not use its body language to trap you into getting bitten. Dogs may be master manipulators when they want their way, but, to our advantage, they do not use manipulation when they intend to attack or bite.

1. Friendly or playful body language:

- ☐ Total body is moving side to side while moving forward in a relaxed way.
- ☐ Face is relaxed while dog is moving.
- ☐ Mouth is opening and closing, relaxed.
- ☐ Dog is bouncing off the ground with body swinging.
- ☐ Front legs are stretched out forward with rear end in the air so that the dog appears to be bowing with its whole body wiggling.

Friendly

- ☐ Dog is moving forward then stopping, while bouncing from side to side.

2. Potentially threatening body language:

- ☐ Dog's head is turned but the dog is still looking at you.
- ☐ Dog is circling you, attempting to attack from behind. *Good time to utilize dog repellent spray or high-pitched sound devices.*
- ☐ Head is carried high or low — high head shows a dominant dog; low head shows a fearful dog.
- ☐ Could be barking or silent; it does not matter which.
- ☐ Mouth is tensed when closed with lips curled tight — could be growling.
- ☐ Front legs are stretched out forward with rear end in the air so that the dog appears to be bowing, *but its body is stiff, not moving.*

Potentially threatening

3. Dangerous body language:

- ☐ A surge of adrenaline will surface, and the dog's body will stiffen. The stiffness will happen whether the dog is moving or still.
- ☐ Hackles (hair along the neck and spine) will rise.
- ☐ Teeth could be showing. Dogs with large muzzle skin will seldom show teeth because they are unable to lift the muzzle skin.
- ☐ Dog maintains direct eye contact that results in tunnel vision. The dog doesn't get distracted by any other movement around it and is unable to hear its owner's commands.

Dangerous

☐ Dog is barking and not moving, trying to warn you to stay away.

☐ The dog's tail could be wagging because it is happy and excited about biting you. A dog with its tail tucked under may bite you out of fear.

☐ The dog makes a fast, direct approach then stops; its next approach may be to bite you. *Good time to utilize dog repellent spray or high-pitched sound devices.*

Keep in mind:

If the attack is imminent and you are knocked down to the ground, curl up in a protective ball. It is not instinctive for a single, domesticated dog, or dogs without a strong killing instinct, to attack its prey when its prey is motionless. This is the same concept that you may have learned about bear attacks. Usually, neither a bear nor a dog will attack a motionless person or prey. This does not hold true for dogs with a strong killing instinct, however. For a description of how they behave, see the chapter on "Dogs That Are Dangerous or Fighters, Because of Breeding or Learned Behavior."

PREPARING YOURSELF
FOR DOG ENCOUNTERS FOR:

CYCLISTS

Any dog can be a threat. All dogs will bite when protecting themselves, their property, and/or their owners. Since dogs can't talk, they will bite to tell you "No," "Get out of here" or "Stop" — even if it's your own dog.

How can you tell the difference between a dog encounter and an attack? In a dog encounter, the dog will confront you but decide not to attack. In an attack the dog has decided to bite you. It's hard to tell when a dog encounter will turn into an attack. Sometimes you surprise a dog and it will attack right away, or it may first try to warn you off. You can't know what any dog will do in the face of stress, so you have to be prepared for both a harmless encounter and an actual attack when you meet a dog. You don't want to injure or kill a harmless dog, but you don't want to get bitten either. The detailed instructions and checklists that follow will help you know what is best to do in a simple encounter and an outright attack.

Photo of Kristy Szczesny and Czar

Five ways dogs behave during a bike encounter:

- A dog's hunting instinct is triggered by the bike's movement, and it will chase you as you ride by.
- A dog will chase you in play.
- A dog will try to stop you by circling you and warning you to stay away.
- If startled, a dog will bite to tell you to stay away.
- A dog will chase you and attempt to knock you off your bike in order to attack you.

When riding your bike, familiarize yourself with the area by checking for:

- ☐ "Beware of Dog" signs
- ☐ dog house, chains, bowls
- ☐ dog feces in yard — the smell may strike you before you actually see them
- ☐ patches of dead grass where the dog's urine has killed it
- ☐ worn track around fence — an indication that the dog is out a lot.
- ☐ If passing by an area you know has a dog, make some noise when approaching the property.
- ☐ If the dog is in a yard where an underground electric fence is confining it don't consider that type of fence a valid means of containment. The dog may get a rush of adrenaline and cross the fence line. The dog's state of aggression will numb its body from the shock and it may bite you.

If owner is present:

- ☐ If the dog is aggressive, keep your eye on the dog and insist the dog be under control, saying, "You *need* to have your dog under control."
- ☐ If you take your eyes off the dog, it may believe it has won the challenge and bite you.
- ☐ Avoid getting angry. Stay on the road or sidewalk. Entering its owner's property may give the dog no other option than to bite you.
- ☐ Warn the owner that, if her dog threatens you again, you will notify Animal Control.
- ☐ If circumstances warrant, notify Animal Control without warning the owner.

Defending yourself during a dog encounter:

- ☐ If a dog is following you, make a mental note where it lives for future encounters.

- ☐ Stop peddling; dogs will bite whatever is moving, so if your legs are moving you may get bitten.

- ☐ If dismounted, keep the bike between you and the dog and evaluate its body language. See the end of this section for a discussion of body language.

- ☐ If dismounted, give it some common commands ("stay," "sit," "down"). This makes the dog think maybe you are in charge.

- ☐ Be careful about giving negative commands ("no," "get out of here"). They may work, but if the dog perceives them as a threat, you may escalate the dog's aggression and get bitten.

- ☐ If you know the dog, relax it by using its name.

- ☐ Look at the dog, but don't stare into its eyes. Look at the top of the dog's head or eyebrows. Looking away may tell the dog it has won the challenge, and it may bite you.

- ☐ Once the dog loses interest in you, move slowly backwards until it is out of sight.

- ☐ Remain calm and confident by taking deep breaths to relax your body. Dogs can sense tension and fear. If the dog senses your fear (and it probably will), it will gain confidence about biting you.

- ☐ Provide the dog room for an escape by not cutting off escape routes such as a door or gate.

- ☐ If you are cornered, wait until the dog loses interest in you. This usually takes only a few minutes, so be patient and wait it out. Then move slowly away.

Defensive techniques during a dog encounter:

- ☐ Stop peddling, or you might attempt to outrun the dog depending on how fast you can go.

- ☐ Carry a high-pitched sound device. See below for how to use the device.

- ☐ Use your bike to strike the dog by holding one end and swinging the other end.

- ☐ Use your helmet to strike the dog instead of your hand. If you injure your hand, you may have a hard time riding away on your bike.

- ☐ Use your tire pump as a striking tool.

- ☐ Squirt your water bottle or spray dog repellent in a figure eight motion towards the dog's head, while riding or at a stop.

☐ Do not throw your bike at the dog. The dog may attack when it sees no barrier (your bike) between it and you.

☐ If an attack is imminent, lay your bike over the dog.

Defending yourself against a dog attack

If the attack is imminent or if you are knocked to the ground, curl up in a ball, protecting your vital organs, face and ears. Do not scream or yell. This will only make the dog more confident. Its survival instinct will surface, and it will attack with renewed force. Once you are on the ground and silent, you are no longer a threat.

If an attack isn't imminent:

☐ Slowly get up if knocked down, listening for the dog.

☐ Be aware of the dog at all times.

☐ As the dog is coming toward you, walk slowly backwards with bike between you and the dog.

☐ Wave a shirt, helmet or sack to present a moving target to distract and confuse the dog.

☐ If bitten, *don't pull away.* This is very difficult to do, but if you pull back, the bite will be more serious because the dog will resist having anything pulled from its mouth and will fight harder to hold on, causing more skin-tearing and deeper wounds.

☐ Spray the dog with repellent. See below for how to use dog repellent spray.

☐ Provide an escape route for the dog so it does not feel cornered.

How to use dog repellent spray:

Whatever brand or type of dog repellent spray you decide to use, read the directions carefully. Check the can regularly to make sure it's still in working order. Do this by shaking the contents vigorously and spraying a small amount. Don't spray too much because repeated testing will use up the spray and leave you with too little when you really need it. If it is cold, make sure the brand you use doesn't freeze. Keep it warm by putting it next to your body.

Dog repellent spray is a nonlethal product that temporarily disorients the dog by surprising it. Dogs don't expect you to reach out and touch them without using your hands. The spray also gives the dog a quick liquid sting and causes temporary eye and nose irritation which distracts it. When it feels the irritation, it will attempt to rub off the substance by pawing at it or rolling on the ground. If you spray the repellent in the dog's mouth, it will immediately begin salivating and be distracted from biting. If the wind is low and the repellent's pressure is at full strength, most sprays can reach up to 12 feet.

In my experience, dog repellent spray works on dogs that have not decided to bite but may do so at any time, such as dogs that are circling you or barking at you but not moving. Don't think the spray is your main line of defense. Dogs that are attacking or are intent on biting you may see it as a threat or a challenge, and in their desire to overcome this challenge will become more aggressive. Such dogs are full of adrenaline and may not feel the spray's effects. When using dog repellent spray:

- ☐ Remember that although you have been told to spray the dog's eyes, that is an almost impossible target to hit. Compared to humans' eyes, dogs have much larger tear ducts and a third eyelid. These assist them in recovering faster. I have been more successful spraying the dog in the mouth. This stimulates the dog's licking reflex, thus stopping it from biting. Also, the mouth is a much larger target.

- ☐ If the dog is biting you or has its face very close to you, try spraying into its nostrils. This will instantly cause maximum irritation and the dog will back off.

- ☐ Spray in a figure eight motion, creating a continuous wall of spray. This will give you a greater chance of hitting some part of the dog's face.

- ☐ Start spraying as soon as you see the dog coming at you, assuming you have the can out and are ready to use it. You must be ready, because a delay will allow the dog to get too close to you or actually begin biting you.

- ☐ Walk backwards keeping an eye on the dog. This creates space and gives you time to think about your other options. See below for how to use striking techniques.

- ☐ Give verbal obedience commands to the dog ("sit," "down" or "stay") as you are walking backwards.

- ☐ While walking backwards, you are also escaping. Some dogs think they have done their jobs when you have gone away from their territory.

High-pitched sound devices:

These emit a high-pitched tone that humans can't hear but dogs can. The device should be used as soon as the dog encounter becomes threatening. These devices cause discomfort to the dog's hearing but have no negative aftereffects. They are about the size of a garage-door opener and fit in the palm of your hand or clip onto your waistband or belt. When you push the activating button, the dog first becomes surprised because it can't tell where the high-pitched sound is coming from. Then it quickly realizes that as it gets closer to you, the sound gets more intense. Being surprised and disturbed by the sound, the dog may not come any closer to you. This device doesn't work on all dogs, but it is an effective protection against dogs that have not yet decided to bite you but could do so at any moment.

Fighting back an attack using striking techniques:

During an attack or if an attack is imminent, you may decide to use striking techniques. Your objective is to destroy the dog's confidence by striking it with dramatic, instant, painful strikes and to survive the encounter with the least amount of injury to yourself. If you think you can't strike the dog effectively, don't use this option. The dog may view your ineffective strikes as a challenge, which will make it fight even harder, thus increasing your chance of injury.

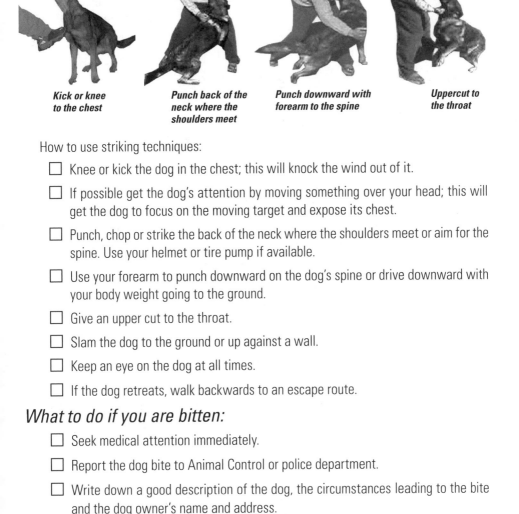

Kick or knee to the chest

Punch back of the neck where the shoulders meet

Punch downward with forearm to the spine

Uppercut to the throat

How to use striking techniques:

☐ Knee or kick the dog in the chest; this will knock the wind out of it.

☐ If possible get the dog's attention by moving something over your head; this will get the dog to focus on the moving target and expose its chest.

☐ Punch, chop or strike the back of the neck where the shoulders meet or aim for the spine. Use your helmet or tire pump if available.

☐ Use your forearm to punch downward on the dog's spine or drive downward with your body weight going to the ground.

☐ Give an upper cut to the throat.

☐ Slam the dog to the ground or up against a wall.

☐ Keep an eye on the dog at all times.

☐ If the dog retreats, walk backwards to an escape route.

What to do if you are bitten:

☐ Seek medical attention immediately.

☐ Report the dog bite to Animal Control or police department.

☐ Write down a good description of the dog, the circumstances leading to the bite and the dog owner's name and address.

☐ Seek legal advice if appropriate.

Loose dogs and stray dogs (notify Animal Control or the local police):

A loose dog or a stray dog has been allowed to determine its own territory. The dog now believes its roaming area, regardless of the size, belongs to it. This makes the dog unpredictable even if it appears friendly. Anyone invading its territory will make the dog protect it, so stay away from all stray dogs and notify Animal Control or the police.

Dogs trained for protection:

While in training to protect its owner and her property, the dog has always been allowed to win. Because of this, the dog's confidence has been so built up that it thinks it can overcome anything a human can give out. Be prepared to divert the dog's attention from you to a target object that it can defeat, such as a hat or sack. While it is attacking the object, it will become vulnerable to your repellent spray, striking techniques or stronger measures.

Dogs not trained for protection:

Similar to a dog trained for protection, a dog not specifically trained for protection will still instinctively protect its house or yard as its territory. It believes that it has won all challenges from people invading its space. After all, you ride by; it barks; you ride on.

The treat myth:

If you carry treats to smooth things over with some dogs, the dogs will see people entering their property as a good thing. The problem arises when strangers see a dog running toward them looking for a treat, and they get confused about what the dog intends. The dog is looking for its treat, but the stranger may well think the dog is about to attack and will hit it, spray it with dog repellent, or use even stronger force. Your treats have created a painful, even fatal, trap for the dog.

How to understand a dog's body language:

Study the body language of dogs you encounter while out cycling. If you have a pet dog, study its body language. What makes a dog excited? What makes it fearful? What stresses it? What does your behavior contribute to the dog's behavior? Familiarize yourself with other types of dogs with different temperaments and from different breeds. Notice especially how the different kinds of dogs look when they are experiencing various emotions ranging from excitement and joy to fear and aggressiveness. Before long you will begin anticipating a particular dog's behavior just by the way it looks, and you will be able to do this for the other types of dogs you have studied.

The dog's eyes are very hard to read. Because they are small, you have to get close up to study them. When the dog is afraid or ready to attack, its eyes glare even if it is excited. When the dog is happy or excited in a friendly way, its eyes look soft. When the dog is sick or sad, its eyes look weak.

Below are the most common body language signs associated with the behaviors you need to know about. Once these become recognizable, you should begin to expand your knowledge by learning the mixed signals dogs give because of undesirable genetics, incorrect training and poor environment. Also, dogs' body language varies according to whether or not they have a tail or have prick or floppy ears.

Remember that the dog's body language does not lie. It does not use its body language to trap you into getting bitten. Dogs may be master manipulators when they want their way, but, to our advantage, they do not use manipulation when they intend to attack or bite.

1. Friendly or playful body language:

☐ Total body is moving side to side while moving forward in a relaxed way.

☐ Face is relaxed while dog is moving.

☐ Mouth is opening and closing, relaxed.

☐ Dog is bouncing off the ground with body swinging.

☐ Front legs are stretched out forward with rear end in the air so that the dog appears to be bowing with its whole body wiggling.

Friendly

☐ Dog is moving forward then stopping, while bouncing from side to side.

2. Potentially threatening body language:

☐ Dog's head is turned but the dog is still looking at you.

☐ Dog is circling you, attempting to attack from behind. *Good time to utilize dog repellent spray or high-pitched sound devices.*

☐ Head is carried high or low — high head shows a dominant dog; low head shows a fearful dog.

Potentially threatening

☐ Could be barking or silent; it does not matter which.

☐ Mouth is tensed when closed with lips curled tight — could be growling.

☐ Front legs are stretched out forward with rear end in the air so that the dog appears to be bowing, *but its body is stiff, not moving.*

3. Dangerous body language:

☐ A surge of adrenaline will surface, and the dog's body will stiffen. The stiffness will happen whether the dog is moving or still.

☐ Hackles (hair along the neck and spine) will rise.

☐ Teeth could be showing. Dogs with large muzzle skin will seldom show teeth because they are unable to lift the muzzle skin.

☐ Dog maintains direct eye contact that results in tunnel vision. The dog doesn't get distracted by any other movement around it and is unable to hear its owner's commands.

☐ Dog is barking and not moving, trying to warn you to stay away.

☐ The dog's tail could be wagging because it is happy and excited about biting you. A dog with its tail tucked under may bite you out of fear.

Dangerous

☐ The dog makes a fast, direct approach then stops; its next approach may be to bite you. *Good time to utilize dog repellent spray or high-pitched sound devices.*

Keep in mind:

If the attack is imminent and you are knocked down to the ground, curl up in a protective ball. It is not instinctive for a single, domesticated dog, or dogs without a strong killing instinct, to attack its prey when its prey is motionless. This is the same concept that you may have learned about bear attacks. Usually, neither a bear nor a dog will attack a motionless person or prey. This does not hold true for dogs with a strong killing instinct, however. For a description of how they behave, see the chapter on "Dogs That Are Dangerous or Fighters, Because of Breeding or Learned Behavior."

VETERINARIANS

Any dog can be a threat. All dogs will bite when protecting themselves, their property, and/or their owners. Since dogs can't talk, they will bite to tell you "No" or "Stop" — even if it's your client's dog.

How can you tell the difference between a dog encounter and an attack? In a dog encounter, the dog will confront you but decide not to attack. In an attack the dog has decided to bite you. It's hard to tell when a dog encounter will turn into an attack. Sometimes you surprise a dog and it will attack right away, or it may first try to warn you off. You can't know what any dog will do in the face of stress, so you have to be prepared for both a harmless

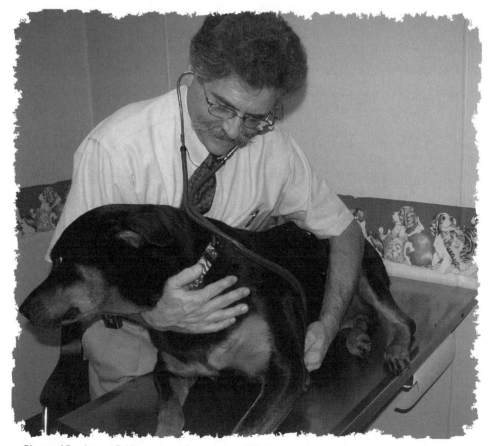

Photo of Dr. James F. Kiomento of Perry Animal Clinic

encounter and an actual attack when you meet a dog. You don't want to injure a harmless dog, but you don't want to get bitten either. The detailed instructions and checklists that follow will help you know what is best to do in a simple encounter and an outright attack.

When treating a dog that the owner says is gentle, remember that the dog may not fight its owner in the way it will fight you. The owner may never have seen his dog behave aggressively or fearfully anywhere else except at the vet's office where it is under stress. If the dog doesn't like having the owner do something to it, the owner usually stops doing it. But as a vet, you must perform your job, and the dog may perceive your persistence as a challenge and retaliate by biting.

How to avoid the five deadly sins of dog encounters:

- Never assume some dogs are friendly. A dog's behavior can change suddenly and without any warning. Dogs under stress are unpredictable.

- Never run from any dog — running triggers the dog's hunting instinct and makes it chase you.

- Never turn your back on any dog. The dog may already be afraid. If you turn away or run, the dog's instinct will tell it to chase you and bite you out of its own fear. Such a dog is a fear-biter.

- Don't depend on the owner to know how her dog will behave under stress.

- Don't stand face to face with a dog during a threat. This will only challenge the dog to a fight.

If you make house calls or farm visits, when arriving at a location check for:

- ☐ "Beware of Dog" signs

- ☐ dog house, chains, bowls

- ☐ sleeping or unalert dog — shake fence or make any noise to alert or wake up dog

- ☐ dog feces in yard — the smell may strike you before you actually see them

- ☐ patches of dead grass where the dog's urine has killed it

- ☐ worn track around fence — an indication that the dog is out a lot.

- ☐ If the dog is tied up and you have to cross its path, don't do so. An aggressive dog may get a burst of strength and break its rope or chain.

- ☐ If the dog is in a yard where an underground electric fence is confining it, don't consider that type of fence a valid means of containment. The dog may get a rush of adrenaline and cross the fence line. The dog's state of aggression will numb its body from the shock and it may bite you.

Vehicles entering the dog owner's yard:

Dogs have learned that a vehicle entering their property signals someone approaching the house. A dog will hear or see the intruder and begin barking, challenging the person and warning him to stay away. The dog often continues barking until the person gets in his vehicle and drives away. When this happens, the dog believes it has done its job by scaring the intruder away. It has won its challenge.

This barking ritual can build an adrenaline high that could make the dog break through a window or door and at worst trigger a bite if the dog gets loose. You will need to be ready to defend yourself against such a dog if this happens. See below for the sections on defensive tactics for dog encounters and attacks.

If a dog continues to bark wildly whenever you drive up, notify the owner of the danger that could result should the dog get loose. If the owner fails to take reasonable measures, such as securing the dog away from windows and doors and making sure the dog is not loose when you arrive, refuse to come to the house.

Why dogs bark at doorbell rings and knocks at the door:

The dog has learned that the doorbell or a knock at the door means someone is on the other side. The dog will bark either because the person is invading its territory or because it is excited about meeting the person. Either way, the dog begins to associate the doorbell or knock with someone arriving. If the dog barks to protect its territory, it will believe it has won once the person leaves, making the dog confident that its bark has scared away the invader. The next time someone knocks or rings the doorbell, the dog will bark more intensely. If the person enters the house, the dog may either continue feeling aggressive about the invader or switch to being friendly because the new person gives it positive attention, touches it and makes friends with it.

If the dog has been barking out of excitement, it learns that when the person comes in, it will be rewarded with a touch and attention. This will make the dog bark more intensely the next time because it gets excited about the idea that the person will enter and give it friendly attention.

Caged or kenneled dog:

Before approaching a caged dog, become familiar with what its body language can tell you. See the last section of this chapter, "How to understand a dog's body language." Also, practice your own non-threatening body language as described in the "Introduction." If the dog is aggressive in the cage or kennel, try using a toy such as a tennis ball to see if the dog will play with it. Play can distract it and direct its energy away from being aggressive.

In approaching a caged dog:

- ☐ Evaluate its body language.
- ☐ Understand that, no matter what you do, there may be some dogs you can't make friends with.
- ☐ Take deep breaths to calm yourself. Dogs will sense your tension and fear.
- ☐ Talk calmly.
- ☐ Give the dog time to calm down.
- ☐ The dog already feels cornered, so be careful reaching into the cage.
- ☐ If the dog is pushed back in the corner, use a hat or something (other than your hand) to touch it to check if it will bite out of fear.
- ☐ Avoid using rolled-up newspaper, which may have been used as a punishment in the past.
- ☐ Don't spend time trying to gain the dog's confidence while it is in the cage. Dogs feel cornered when they are in a cage; so remove the dog from the cage and work on establishing trust out in the open.

Removing the dog from a kennel or cage:

- ☐ Don't hesitate when placing a slip lead on the dog.
- ☐ If the dog resists, distract it by having a second person with a treat to help secure the slip lead.
- ☐ Put on the slip lead while the dog is eating the treat.
- ☐ The dog may have never been on a leash, so expect some protesting.
- ☐ Remain still if the dog fights against the leash.
- ☐ If the dog is dangerous, use a snare and/or a three-foot square piece of quarter-inch plywood with an oval handhold (edges smoothed) cut in the top. With this you can protect your legs while pushing the dog back. Use the snare and plywood together or individually, depending on what best suits the case.

Using the snare (sometimes called control pole or rabies stick):

A snare is a pole with a noose at one end that is used to restrain loose or dangerous dogs safely. When tightened, it applies even pressure around the dog's neck so the dog doesn't injure itself or others. The snare's pole usually has a plastic coating next to the noose so the dog can bite it without injuring its teeth. However, using a snare may make some dogs respond by becoming instantly aggressive and fighting you. If this happens, remain still until the dog stops fighting. For a full discussion of what arouses aggressive dogs and how to handle them, see the chapter for "Parents," the sections on what makes dogs aggressive and how to handle aggressive dogs.

When using the snare:

- ☐ Inspect the snare regularly — depending on how much you use it, you may need to replace the noose fairly often.
- ☐ Before using the snare, loosen the noose so it hangs free.
- ☐ Keep the snare at your side and down — don't hold it high or behind you. Holding it high may make it look like a weapon, and keeping it behind you may surprise the dog when you present it.
- ☐ Use both hands on the pole when putting the noose around the dog's neck and apply firm tension.
- ☐ Don't try to lift the dog with the snare pole; you could injure its neck.
- ☐ For large or strong dogs have a second person push the dog forward with the plywood board, while you handle the snare in front with two hands and move the dog into the cage or kennel.
- ☐ Never pull or jerk on the pole to get the dog to move. Step behind the dog, and it will usually walk away from you, thus walking forward.
- ☐ If the dog still refuses to move, use a three-foot square piece of plywood to push the dog forward. Walk next to or behind the dog.
- ☐ If the dog fights, remain still and allow it to fight itself.
- ☐ If you are alone with a large or strong dog, keep two hands on the pole while leading the dog into the kennel or cage.
- ☐ Once the dog is in the kennel or cage, place your foot on the door while pressing the door against the pole to prevent the dog from escaping. When removing the snare from the dog, use one hand to loosen and remove it, pull the snare quickly out of the door and with the other hand lock the cage door.
- ☐ If you are putting a strange dog into your truck or van, lay down a plank for the dog to walk on in order to get into the vehicle.

Bite prevention techniques:

- ☐ Distract the dog with a massage, squeeze or scratch before an injection or nail clipping.
- ☐ Be familiar with stress signals such as yawning, shaking, licking lips, looking away or scratching.
- ☐ Don't trust the owner — trust the dog's body language.

☐ Avoid eye-to-eye contact. If you make eye contact, distract the dog with a snap of your fingers or similar noise. This will make the dog look away and lose the challenge without any conflict.

☐ Be prepared for the few dogs for whom a tranquilizer will not work. See next section on "Tranquilizers."

☐ Remember, any force you use may create aggression or fear for future visits.

☐ Be aware that muzzled dogs can still be dangerous. For a discussion of using muzzles, see the chapter for "Parents."

Tranquilizers:

Dogs that normally would not bite are at higher risk to bite while tranquilized. The tranquilizer relaxes the dog's motor functions and causes disorganized thinking, making it unpredictable. When tranquilized, the dog appears to be drunk and is not thinking or behaving normally.

Using the cone collar (also called "Elizabethan collar"):

This collar is plastic and snaps or ties together around the dog's neck. It extends past the muzzle and is ordinarily used to prevent the dog from irritating or reopening a wound. It prevents the dog's head from having full motion and access to the body. When used in conjunction with a muzzle, the cone collar provides the maximum protection. Many local pet supply stores carry cone collars.

When you first put the cone collar on, the dog will attempt to remove it by dropping its head and pawing it off. You should get the dog comfortable with it so it doesn't see the collar as a source of stress or a form of punishment. If you know in advance that you will be using a cone collar on the dog, have its owner prepare the dog by following the steps outlined below. Otherwise, you may have to go through these steps while the dog is at your office.

Preparing the dog for wearing the cone collar:

☐ Use treats to get the dog to like it. Put it on and off the dog, giving it a treat both when putting the collar on and taking it off.

☐ If the dog is not treat motivated, go through basic obedience commands with the collar on. Don't correct the dog for pawing at the collar, but rather give the dog an obedience command and correct it for disobedience, such as stopping and pawing while heeling.

☐ While walking on lead make right, left or about turns (U-turns) whenever the dog attempts to use its paws to remove the collar. By turning you're making the dog's front legs drop so it is harder for it to reach up and paw.

☐ Calm the dog by stroking or massaging its body.

☐ Walk at a faster than normal speed, making the dog move its feet faster.

When to use the cone collar:

➡ To prevent chewing and biting in puppies and adult dogs.

➡ To make draining the anal glands safer for the veterinarian or owner.

➡ To make nail trimming safer.

➡ To keep the dog from eating bad things (socks, houseplants, feces, etc.).

➡ To stop play biting.

➡ To prevent dog fighting, but only if the other dog has a cone collar on.

➡ To prevent the dog from irritating a wound.

When giving something to a person with a dog or taking something from him:

☐ Have the person come to you; this will make the dog invade your space instead of you invading its. If you invade a dog's personal space or it perceives your coming towards it as a threat, it may bite you.

☐ Have the person take the object while you hold the object close to you. Your hand reaching out could be perceived as a threat.

☐ When leaving, do not turn your back on the dog and walk away. Instead, either walk slowly backwards to a safe distance while always keeping your eye on the dog or allow the owner and dog to leave first.

☐ If the dog becomes aggressive at any time, walk backwards to create space and place the object somewhere else. Tell the owner to stop coming toward you.

☐ On a house call or farm visit, if the screen door is the only door visible and the dog is jumping on the door, place your foot on the door and your hand on the outside of door to make sure the dog doesn't force the door open. If the door is broken shout for owner.

☐ Don't give or receive anything from a child when a dog is present. Dogs know children are vulnerable and may see them as property which needs protecting. A child can bond so closely to her dog that the dog will instinctively protect her as if the child were its own.

Expressing anal glands:

Draining the anal glands and clipping nails place veterinarians at the highest risk of getting bitten. The glands are surrounded by many nerve endings and touching them may cause the dog enough pain to make it protest by biting. Because dogs smell these glands when meeting each other and receive signals about the other dog's strengths and weaknesses, they are touchy about having their anal glands handled. Dominant dogs perceive that anyone who handles this area is testing their dominance and will respond by challenging that person.

The glands contain a foul-smelling, brown or milky-brown secretion that is usually expressed automatically with the dog's feces, if the dog is receiving a proper diet and exercise. If the dog doesn't automatically secrete the glands' contents, they may have to be drained by someone else in order to relieve the pressure they exert.

Using surgical gloves, apply gradual, even pressure against the gland with your index finger. Drain both glands' contents onto a tissue or rag. When you begin doing this, the dog may empty the glands involuntarily due to fear or stress. Draining the anal glands can be done by owners, groomers or veterinarians. If done incorrectly, emptying the anal glands by hand may cause the dog a lot of pain. Below are some tips that will make the task easier for you and the dog and help prevent a struggle or a possible dog bite.

Tips for cleaning anal glands (for veterinarians and owners):

☐ Ask the owner for a history of the dog's behavior during this treatment; this will let you know how much assistance you will need.

☐ Empty the glands during a warm bath.

☐ Place your hand with latex glove in warm water.

☐ Lubricate the latex glove.

☐ Use a warm rag to relax the anus.

☐ Distract the dog by massaging another part of its body.

☐ Use a second person to hold or secure the dog's head.

☐ Raise the back feet off the ground and have a second person empty the glands. This puts the dog off balance and makes it unable to bite.

☐ Tell the owner to look for any blood in the discharge. If blood is present the owner should take the dog to a veterinarian.

Nail trimming:

As with expressing the anal glands, nail trimming leads to a lot of bites to veterinarians. For the veterinarian's safety, the dog's owner must teach it that touching its feet will not lead to pain. A dog's nails have many nerve endings and blood vessels. If its nails are clipped too close causing pain and bleeding, the nicest dog will bite. In this section I will give suggestions for both owners and veterinarians about how to clip a dog's nails without using force.

How an owner can prepare the dog for nail trimming:

Owners can help veterinarians with nail trimming by getting the dog accustomed to having its paws touched without any stress. Either the veterinarian or a knowledgeable staff member should instruct new puppy owners how to accustom the puppy to having its feet handled. Owners should touch, tickle and squeeze the puppy's entire paw and massage its feet daily. Touch the puppy's nails regularly. This will reduce the puppy's anxiety level when the time comes to trim its nails. Veterinarians recommend the same procedure for mature dogs that are not used to having their nails trimmed.

At first, try trimming the nails with a nail file instead of a clipper. Don't wait until the nails are so long it becomes painful for the dog to walk on them or to have them trimmed. Most important, obedience train your dog. This will help control your dog if it decides to rebel halfway into nail trimming.

Nail trimming supplies:

Nail trimmers: The two types of nail trimmers are: guillotine style, which cut up and down and scissors style, which cut sideways, similarly to a pair of scissors. The choice is up to you, but be sure the trimmer is sharp and of good quality.

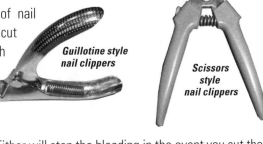

Guillotine style nail clippers

Scissors style nail clippers

Styptic powder or cornstarch: Either will stop the bleeding in the event you cut the nail's quick. The quick, located in the nail, contains sensitive nerve endings and a blood vein. In nails that are light, the quick is pink and easy to see. In darker nails, it can be harder to see. If you are unsure about where the quick is, trim only the nail tips. Some dogs bleed fairly easily, and even a small nick can produce quite a bit of blood.

Remember, the quick grows with the nail, so you should trim your dog's nails on a regular basis, or walk your dog on rough surfaces such as sidewalks and tennis courts to wear the nails down to the desired length.

Trimming the nail: Grasp the paw with your entire hand. Apply pressure with your thumb toward the dog's paw so the nail protrudes. This will expose the nail to be trimmed, making it easier to target. Trim the nail straight up and down, or angled away from the nail.

The problem with forceful nail trimming: A method commonly used is to have someone hold down the dog or reach over the dog and put it in a head lock. Either way, the dog is fighting and learning to hate this. The more the dog fights, the more you have to fight. If the fight escalates, you will need more people to control the dog.

From a training and psychological viewpoint, forced nail trimming creates a battle of wills. It also makes you dependent on that method because you have taught the dog to fight nail trimming instead of cooperating in it. Worst of all, your dog has learned that fighting and struggling are integral parts of its relationship with you and with other humans and that, when it doesn't want to do something, it can expect the human pack (you and your family) to fight to make it obey. If you are alone with your dog and have to struggle with it over nail trimming or anything else, you will almost certainly lose the battle. Such defeats reinforce the dog's dominance over you, and your dog will start to believe it can win any battle.

The effect a negative nail trimming experience has on your dog is terrible. When you try to touch you dog's nails or paws, it will get a surge of anxiety and quickly pull away, snap at you or bite you. If you have to resort to the pin and hold method of nail clipping, you will be better off not clipping your dog's nails at all. Take it for a walk on cement or play fetch on a tennis court. This will file down your dog's nails naturally.

Several nail trimming methods that require no force:

The first two methods require an assistant.

1. Cradling: This method works well with small dogs and young dogs. Hold the dog up, even with your chest across your body so that its feet dangle. Have someone reach underneath the dog's feet and trim its nails. Dogs like  this because having you hold them makes them feel secure. You avoid a struggle because your dog has a very hard time fighting when its feet are not touching the ground.

2. Standing the dog on two feet: Hold the dog up so it is standing on two feet with its back against your chest. This puts your dog's feet out in front, giving your assistant an easy target. This works only for the front feet, but those nails need trimming twice as often as the back nails. For the back nails, use one of the other methods.

3. Elevating the dog: Place your dog on a high table so it will not be able to jump or fight. The dog is standing at your eye level, and you will be able to trim the nails.

The next five sections are applicable to veterinarians' clients. You may want to use them to educate clients when appropriate.

Defensive tactics against a dog encounter:

- ☐ Do not run; you will only cause the dog's biting instinct to surface.
- ☐ If a dog is following you, stop and evaluate. The dog may just want to smell you.
- ☐ Stop and stand sideways, so the dog doesn't think you are challenging it.
- ☐ Avoid quick movement. The dog could be nervous and a quick movement may trigger fear-biting.
- ☐ If the dog is coming towards you, move backwards and sideways, keeping an eye on the dog. This gives you space and time to react.
- ☐ Give it some common commands ("stay," "sit," "down"). This makes the dog think maybe you are in charge.
- ☐ Be careful about giving negative commands ("no," "get out of here"). They may work, but if a dog perceives them as a threat you may escalate the dog's aggression and get bitten.
- ☐ Look at the dog, but don't stare into its eyes. Look at the top of its head or at its eyebrows. Looking away may tell the dog it has won the challenge, and it may bite you.
- ☐ If you know the dog, relax it by using its name.
- ☐ Once the dog loses interest in you, move slowly backwards until you are out of its sight.
- ☐ Provide the dog room for an escape by not cutting off escape routes such as a door or gate.
- ☐ Remain calm by taking deep breaths. This will calm your body; dogs can sense tension and fear. If the dog senses your fear (and it probably will), it will gain confidence about biting you.
- ☐ If cornered, remain still and wait until the dog loses interest. This usually takes only a few minutes, so be patient. Then move slowly away.

Defending yourself against a dog attack: stop, drop and curl:

If the attack is imminent, fall on the ground and curl up in a ball, protecting your vital organs, face and ears. Do not scream or yell. This will only make the dog more confident. Its survival instinct will surface, and it will attack with renewed force. Once you are on the ground and silent, you are no longer a threat.

Listen to hear if the dog is still there. If it is but is not sounding threatening, stand up slowly while keeping an eye on the dog.

How to defend yourself if an attack is threatened but not imminent:

☐ Stop and stand sideways, so the dog doesn't think you're challenging it.

☐ Remain aware of where the dog is at all times.

☐ Carry a high-pitched sound device. See below for how to use the device.

☐ As the dog is running toward you, walk backwards and sideways, so you can keep an eye on the dog, being ready to hit it if you have to.

☐ Turning around and walking away while looking over your shoulder at the dog may make it bite you out of fear. Turning your back on the dog also keeps you from making a good solid hit at it if you have to.

☐ Wave a shirt or hat to present a moving target and to distract and confuse the dog.

☐ If the dog is biting you, spray dog repellent or strike it. See below for how to use dog repellent spray and techniques for striking the dog.

☐ Use defensive options in escalating order: verbal commands, dog repellent spray, striking techniques.

☐ If bitten *don't pull away.* This is very difficult to do, but if you pull away, the bite will be much more serious because the dog will resist having anything pulled from its mouth and will fight harder to hold on, causing more skin-tearing and deeper wounds.

☐ If you fall or are knocked down, curl up in a protective ball as outlined at the beginning of this section.

☐ Listen for the dog and stand up slowly.

How to use dog repellent spray:

Whatever brand or type of dog repellent spray you decide to use, read the directions carefully. Check the can regularly to make sure it's still in working order. Do this by shaking the contents vigorously and spraying a small amount. Don't spray too much because repeated testing will use up the spray and leave you with too little when you really need it. If it is cold, make sure the brand you use doesn't freeze. Keep it warm by putting it next to your body.

Dog repellent spray is a nonlethal product that temporarily disorients the dog by surprising it, because the dog doesn't expect you to be able to touch it without coming close and using your hands. The spray also gives the dog a quick liquid sting and causes temporary eye and nose irritation which distracts it. When the dog feels the irritation, it will attempt to rub off the substance by pawing at it or rolling on the ground. If you spray the repellent in the dog's mouth, it will immediately begin salivating and be distracted from biting. If the wind is low and the repellent's pressure is at full strength, most sprays can reach up to 12 feet.

In my experience, dog repellent spray works on dogs that have not decided to bite but may do so at any time, such as dogs that are circling you or barking at you but not moving. Don't think the spray is your main line of defense. Dogs that are attacking or are intent on biting you may see it as a threat or a challenge, and in their desire to overcome this challenge will become more aggressive. Such dogs are full of adrenaline and may not feel the effects of the spray. When using dog repellent spray:

- [ ] Remember that although you have been told to spray the dog's eyes, that is an almost impossible target to hit. Compared to humans' eyes, dogs have much larger tear ducts and a third eyelid. These assist them in recovering faster. I have been more successful spraying the dog in the mouth. This stimulates the dog's licking reflex, thus stopping it from biting. Also, the mouth is a much larger target.

- [ ] If the dog is biting you or has its face very close to you, try spraying into its nostrils. This will instantly cause maximum irritation, and the dog will back off.

- [ ] Spray in a figure eight motion, creating a continuous wall of spray. This will give you a greater chance of hitting some part of the dog's face.

- [ ] Start spraying as soon as you see the dog coming at you, assuming you have the can out and are ready to use it. You must be ready, because a delay will allow the dog to get too close to you or actually begin biting you.

- [ ] Walk backwards keeping an eye on the dog. This creates space and gives you time to think about your other options. See below for how to use striking techniques.

- [ ] Give verbal obedience commands to the dog ("sit," "down" or "stay") as you are walking backwards.

- [ ] While walking backwards, you are also escaping. Some dogs think they have done their jobs when you have gone away from their territory.

High-pitched sound devices:

These emit a high-pitched tone that humans can't hear but dogs can. The device should be used as soon as the dog encounter becomes threatening. These devices cause discomfort to the dog's hearing but have no negative aftereffects. They are about the size of a garage-door opener and fit in the palm of your hand or clip onto your waistband or belt. When you push the activating button, the dog first becomes surprised because it can't tell where the high-pitched sound is coming from. Then it quickly realizes that as it gets closer to you, the sound gets more intense. Being surprised and disturbed by the sound, the dog may not come any closer to you. This device doesn't work on all dogs, but it is an effective protection against dogs that have not yet decided to bite you but could do so at any moment.

Fighting back an attack using striking techniques:

During an attack or if an attack is imminent, you may decide to use striking techniques. Your objective is to destroy the dog's confidence by striking it with dramatic, instant, painful strikes and to survive the encounter with the least amount of injury to yourself. If you think you can't strike the dog effectively, don't use this option. The dog may view your ineffective strikes as a challenge, which will make it fight even harder, thus increasing your chance of injury.

| Kick or knee to the chest | Punch back of the neck where the shoulders meet | Punch downward with forearm to the spine | Uppercut to the throat |

How to use striking techniques:

☐ Knee or kick the dog in the chest; this will knock the wind out of it.

☐ If possible get the dog's attention by moving something over your head; this will get the dog to focus on the moving target and expose its chest.

☐ Punch, chop or strike the back of the neck where the shoulders meet, or aim for the spine. Use any object that will make an impact.

☐ Use your forearm to punch downward on the dog's spine or drive downward with your body weight going to the ground.

☐ Give an upper cut to the throat.

☐ Slam the dog to the ground or up against a wall.

☐ Keep an eye on the dog at all times.

☐ If the dog retreats, walk backwards to an escape route.

Loose dogs and stray dogs (notify Animal Control or the police):

When making house calls or farm visits you may come across stray dogs and dogs that protect their owners' property. This and the following two sections are intended to prepare you for such encounters. A loose dog or a stray dog has been allowed to determine its own territory. The dog now believes its roaming area, regardless of the size, belongs to it. This makes the dog unpredictable even if it appears friendly. Anyone invading its territory will make the dog protect it, so stay away from all stray dogs and notify Animal Control or the police.

Dogs trained for protection:

While in training to protect its owner and her property, the dog has always been allowed to win. Because of this, the dog's confidence has been so built up that it thinks it can overcome anything a human can give out. Be prepared to divert the dog's attention from you to a target object that it can defeat, such as a hat or sack. While it is attacking the object, it will become vulnerable to your repellent spray, striking techniques or stronger measures.

Dogs not trained for protection:

Similar to a dog trained for protection, a dog not specifically trained for protection will still instinctively protect its house or yard as its territory. It believes that it has won all challenges from people invading its space. After all, you enter its territory; it barks; you leave.

Using treats:

Although I do not usually recommend using treats to pacify dogs, for veterinarians they can be very helpful in smoothing things over with some dogs. In order to get quick results, use a very tasty treat such as cooked chicken or liver, not the normal dry biscuit.

How to understand a dog's body language:

Study the body language of dogs you encounter during work, as well as your own pets. What makes the dog excited? What makes it fearful? What stresses it? What does your behavior contribute to the dog's behavior? Familiarize yourself with other types of dogs with different temperaments and from different breeds. Notice especially how the different kinds of dogs look when they are experiencing various emotions ranging from excitement and joy to fear and aggressiveness. Before long you will begin anticipating a particular dog's behaviors just by the way it looks, and you will be able to do this for the other types of dogs you have studied.

The dog's eyes are very hard to read. Because they are small, you have to get close up to study them. When the dog is afraid or ready to attack, its eyes glare, even if it is excited about biting you. When the dog is happy or excited in a friendly way, its eyes look soft. When the dog is sick or sad, its eyes look weak.

Below are the most common body language signs associated with the behaviors you need to know about. Once these become recognizable, you should begin to expand your knowledge by learning the mixed signals dogs give because of undesirable genetics, incorrect training and poor environment. Also, dogs' body language varies according to whether or not they have a tail or have prick or floppy ears.

Remember that the dog's body language does not lie. It does not use its body language to trap you into getting bitten. Dogs may be master manipulators when they want their way, but, to our advantage, they do not use manipulation when they intend to attack or bite.

1. Friendly or playful body language:

☐ Total body is moving side to side while moving forward in a relaxed way.

☐ Face is relaxed while dog is moving.

☐ Mouth is opening and closing, relaxed.

☐ Dog is bouncing off the ground with body swinging.

Friendly

☐ Front legs are stretched out forward with rear end in the air so that the dog appears to be bowing with its whole body wiggling.

☐ Dog is moving forward then stopping, while bouncing from side to side.

2. Potentially threatening body language:

☐ Dog's head is turned but the dog is still looking at you.

☐ Dog is circling you, attempting to attack from behind. *Good time to utilize dog repellent spray or high-pitched sound devices.*

☐ Head is carried high or low — high head shows a dominant dog; low head shows a fearful dog.

☐ Could be barking or silent; it does not matter which.

Potentially threatening

☐ Mouth is tensed when closed with lips curled tight — could be growling.

☐ Front legs are stretched out forward with rear end in the air so that the dog appears to be bowing, *but its body is stiff, not moving.*

3. Dangerous body language:

☐ A surge of adrenaline will surface, and the dog's body will stiffen. The stiffness will happen whether the dog is moving or still.

☐ Hackles (hair along the neck and spine) will rise.

☐ Teeth could be showing. Dogs with large muzzle skin will seldom show teeth because they are unable to lift the muzzle skin.

☐ Dog maintains direct eye contact that results in tunnel vision. The dog doesn't get distracted by any other movement around it and is unable to hear its owner's commands.

☐ Dog is barking and not moving, trying to warn you to stay away.

Dangerous

☐ The dog's tail could be wagging because it is happy and excited about biting you. A dog with its tail tucked under may bite you out of fear.

☐ The dog makes a fast, direct approach then stops; its next approach may be to bite you. *Good time to utilize dog repellent spray or high-pitched sound devices.*

Keep in mind:

If the attack is imminent and you are knocked down to the ground, curl up in a protective ball. It is not instinctive for a single, domesticated dog, or dogs without a strong killing instinct, to attack its prey when its prey is motionless. This is the same concept that you may have learned about bear attacks. Usually, neither a bear nor a dog will attack a motionless person or prey. This does not hold true for dogs with a strong killing instinct, however. For a description of how they behave, see the chapter on "Dogs That Are Dangerous or Fighters, Because of Breeding or Learned Behavior."

GROOMERS
AND OWNERS WHO TAKE THEIR DOGS
TO GROOMERS

Groomers have a higher risk of getting bitten than any other professional who works with dogs. Dog owners who take their puppies or dogs to a groomer must ensure the groomer's safety by preparing the dog for grooming. This includes properly socializing the dog and teaching it basic obedience. The groomer should not have to socialize or train any dog that comes in for grooming. The dog is there for only a short time. If the groomer has to both groom and train the dog, she may have to rush the experience, causing the dog stress. Under stress, the dog may become aggressive or fearful. In either case, it may bite the groomer. A good groomer is a wizard at understanding and coping with all kinds of behavior that dogs exhibit, but unless the owner does her part in preparing the dog, the groomer will be at risk for getting bitten.

Advice for owners:

How to choose a groomer: Choosing the right groomer is just as vital as choosing a good trainer. Both of these professionals will have an impact on your dog's temperament that will affect other facets of the dog's relationship with you and your family. A bad groomer can make your dog fearful and unpredictable when faced with future handling by other people, including you. Here are some ways to evaluate a groomer:

- ☐ Understand the groomer's motivation. Groomers make their money by the number of dogs they groom, so they have a strong incentive to groom a lot of dogs fairly quickly. Make sure you look for a groomer who will take time to groom your dog. Avoid groomers who, in order to meet a tight schedule, rush through each dog's grooming. This may well result in mistakes that cause pain or injuries such as razor burns or cuts. Cuts may also result from poor quality grooming tools.

- ☐ Don't make price the main factor. If you have to save money on grooming do it by learning how to take care of your dog's coat between professional groomings. That way the groomer won't have to do a lot of extra work just to get your dog ready to be groomed. Also, if your dog is badly matted, it may get razor burns or cuts.

- ☐ Inspect the grooming area before coming into it with your dog. Is it clean? Is there good, temporary dog housing, such as crates for each dog?

- ☐ Request to observe other dogs being groomed. Most groomers will not allow you to watch your own dog being groomed because your presence might excite and distract it.

- ☐ Ask the groomer for references — people whose dogs they have groomed for more than a year. If you can't get references, ask friends or a professional dog trainer whom they would recommend.

If a groomer sends your dog home with cuts or razor burns, find out what has caused them. Some dogs have very sensitive skin and get clipper burns around the eyes and genitals. Some wiggle uncontrollably, and others are so matted it's almost impossible to clip them without causing cuts or burns. If the groomer doesn't address such problems in a professional manner or won't cooperate with you to make the grooming less difficult, don't go back to that groomer.

Owners' responsibilities:

- ☐ Before the grooming appointment, bring in the puppy or dog to get acquainted with the place and the groomer.

- ☐ Make the first grooming visit short.

- ☐ Accustom your dog to behaving well during grooming early in its life. Don't wait until the dog's behavior gets so bad that the groomer has to spend a lot of extra time with the dog. This will only cause more stress for both dog and groomer.

☐ Socialize your dog to the grooming process by taking it to meet the groomer before its first appointment and following the groomer's suggestions about how to groom your dog at home.

☐ Teach your dog common obedience commands — especially the "stay." It will be especially helpful if your dog will stay in the "down," "sit" or "stand."

Groomer's checklist for signs of stress in the dog being groomed:

☐ yawning

☐ excessive itching

☐ excessive licking of lips

☐ shaking (but some dogs will always shake when being groomed)

☐ closed, tense mouth

☐ pulled-back ears

☐ tucked under tail.

If the dog continually exhibits any of these signs, give it a break from grooming. Let it rest in a crate for a while or, better still, take it for a walk.

Groomer's responsibilities:

☐ Become familiar with different kinds of training methods. Know when to use them and on which dogs. Ideally, you shouldn't have to train a dog while grooming it, but in case you get a dog that becomes disobedient under the stress of grooming, some basic training work may be essential.

☐ Constantly review the dog's body language for signs of stress.

☐ Don't trust the owner about whether or not the dog will bite. All dogs will bite under stress.

☐ Be honest with the owner about the dog's behavior. If necessary, to make your job safer, talk with the owner about how to remedy any behavior problems in the dog.

☐ If the dog struggles during grooming, allow it to fight itself and lose. Don't discipline the dog for struggling. Just remain still, don't let it escape and let it teach itself not to fight.

☐ Don't force the dog. If it moves around a lot you may accidentally cut it or give it razor burn. Be patient and take your time. If necessary charge the owner more for the extra time and trouble. Explain this to the owner and suggest remedies for the dog's behavior so the owner can avoid extra charges in the future.

☐ Avoid tranquilizing the dog; this may make it difficult to read the dog's body language. A tranquilized dog may well bite despite the tranquilizer.

☐ Muzzle the dog if you have to, but remember, a muzzled dog can still be a threat. For a discussion of how to use the muzzle, see the section on muzzles in the "Parents" chapter.

Tranquilizers:

Dogs that normally would not bite may be at higher risk for biting while tranquilized. The tranquilizer relaxes the dog's motor functions and causes disorganized thinking, making it unpredictable. When tranquilized, the dog appears to be drunk and is not thinking or behaving normally.

Nevertheless, most groomers report that tranquilizing, *as a last resort*, usually works well for difficult dogs. Good professional groomers will have a difficult dog's veterinarian prescribe a tranquilizer and will have it on hand for grooming that dog.

Some reasons why dogs bite groomers:

☐ Groomer forces the dog to complete the grooming session despite signals from the dog that it is becoming stressed.

☐ Dog becomes fearful.

☐ Dog resorts to biting as the only way to tell the groomer, "No, stop!"

☐ Dog does not respect common obedience commands.

☐ The dog is a dominant type and sees grooming as a challenge to its dominance.

If you are grooming a dog that constantly tries to bite you no matter what you do, you may need to use a cone collar. See the section on cone collars in the chapter for "Veterinarians."

Expressing anal glands:

Draining the anal glands and clipping nails place groomers at the highest risk of getting bitten. The glands are surrounded by many nerve endings and touching them may cause the dog enough pain to make it protest by biting. Because dogs smell these glands when meeting each other and receive signals about the other dog's strengths and weaknesses, they are touchy about having their anal glands handled. Dominant dogs perceive that anyone who handles this area is testing their dominance and will respond by challenging that person.

The glands contain a foul-smelling, brown or milky-brown secretion that is usually expressed automatically with the dog's feces, if the dog is receiving a proper diet and exercise. If the dog doesn't automatically secrete the glands' contents, they may have to be drained by someone else in order to relieve the pressure they exert.

Using surgical gloves, apply gradual even pressure against the gland with your index finger. Drain both glands' contents onto a tissue or rag. When you begin doing this, the dog may empty the glands involuntarily due to fear or stress. Draining the anal glands can be done by owners, groomers or veterinarians. If done incorrectly, emptying the anal glands by hand may cause the dog a lot of pain. Before attempting this procedure, owners and groomers should have a veterinarian show them how to perform it without causing excessive pain to the dog. Below are some tips that will make the task easier for you and the dog, preventing a struggle or possible dog bite.

Tips for cleaning anal glands (for groomers and owners):

- ☐ Ask the owner for a history of the dog's behavior during this treatment; this will let you know how much assistance you will need.
- ☐ Empty the glands during a warm bath.
- ☐ Place your hand with latex glove in warm water.
- ☐ Lubricate the latex glove.
- ☐ Use a warm rag to relax the anus.
- ☐ Distract the dog by massaging another part of its body.
- ☐ Use a second person to hold or secure the dog's head.
- ☐ Raise the back feet off the ground and have a second person empty the glands. This puts the dog off balance and makes it unable to bite.
- ☐ Tell the owner to look for any blood in the discharge. If blood is present the owner should take the dog to a veterinarian.

Nail trimming:

As with expressing the anal glands, a lot of bites take place during nail trimming. For the groomer's safety, the dog's owner must teach it that touching its feet will not lead to pain. A dog's nails have many nerve endings and blood vessels. If its nails are clipped too close causing pain and bleeding, the nicest dog will bite. In this section I will give suggestions for both owners and groomers about how to clip a dog's nails without using force.

How an owner can prepare the dog for nail trimming:

Owners can help groomers with nail trimming by getting the dog accustomed to having its paws touched without any stress. If possible, touch, tickle and squeeze the entire paw and massage your dog's feet daily. This will reduce its anxiety level when the time comes to trim its nails. Touch the dog's nails regularly. Try trimming them with a nail file instead of a clipper. Don't wait until the nails are so long it becomes painful to the dog to walk on them or have them trimmed. Most important, obedience train your dog. This will help control your dog if it decides to rebel halfway into nail trimming.

Nail trimming supplies:

Nail trimmers: The two types of nail trimmers are: guillotine style, which cut up and down and scissors style, which cut sideways, similarly to a pair of scissors. The choice is up to you, but be sure the trimmer is sharp and of good quality.

Guillotine style nail clippers

Scissors style nail clippers

Styptic powder or cornstarch: Either will stop the bleeding in the event you cut the nail's quick. The quick, located in the nail, contains sensitive nerve endings and a blood vein. In nails that are light, the quick is pink and easy to see. In darker nails, it can be harder to see. If you are unsure about where the quick is, trim only the nail tips. Some dogs bleed fairly easily, and even a small nick can produce quite a bit of blood.

Remember, the quick grows with the nail, so you should trim your dog's nails on a regular basis, or walk your dog on rough surfaces such as sidewalks and tennis courts to wear the nails down to the desired length.

Trimming the nail: Grasp the paw with your entire hand. Apply pressure with your thumb toward the dog's paw so the nail protrudes. This will expose the nail to be trimmed, making it easier to target. Trim the nail straight up and down, or angled away from the nail.

The problem with forceful nail trimming:

A method commonly used is to have someone hold down the dog or reach over the dog and put it in a head lock. Either way, the dog is fighting and learning to hate this. The more the dog fights, the more you have to fight. If the fight escalates, you will need more people to control the dog.

From a training and psychological viewpoint, forced trimming creates a battle of wills. It also makes you dependent on that method because you have taught the dog to fight nail trimming instead of cooperating in it. Worst of all, your dog has learned that fighting and struggling are integral parts of its relationship with you and with other humans and that, when it doesn't want to do something, it can expect the human pack (you and your family) to fight to make it obey. If you are alone with your dog and have to struggle with it over nail trimming or anything else, you will almost certainly lose the battle. Such defeats reinforce the dog's dominance over you, and your dog will start to believe it can win any battle.

The effect a negative nail trimming experience has on your dog is terrible. When you try to touch you dog's nails or paws, it will get a surge of anxiety and quickly pull away, snap at you or bite you. If you have to resort to the pin and hold method of nail clipping, you will be better off not clipping your dog's nails at all. Take it for a walk on cement or play fetch on a tennis court. This will file down your dog's nails naturally.

Several nail trimming methods that require no force:

The first two methods require an assistant.

1. Cradling: This method works well with small dogs and young dogs. Hold the dog up, even with your chest across your body so that its feet dangle. Have someone reach underneath the dog's feet and trim its nails. Dogs like this because having you hold them makes them feel secure. You avoid a struggle because your dog has a very hard time fighting when its feet are not touching the ground.

2. Standing the dog on two feet: Hold the dog up so it is standing on two feet with its back against your chest. This puts your dog's feet out in front, giving your assistant an easy target. This works only for the front feet, but those nails require trimming twice as often as the hind feet. Use one of the other methods for hind feet.

3. Elevating the dog: Place your dog on a high table so it will not be able to jump or fight. The dog is standing at your eye level, and you will be able to trim the nails.

Brushing the dog, advice for owners and groomers:

Brushing is an activity associated with bonding. Some dogs have a difficult time allowing people outside of their pack to brush (bond with) them. Make sure you as the owner get the dog used to being brushed before its first visit to a groomer.

Brushing tips for owners:

- ☐ Brush the dog when it is calm, such as after it has eaten or during a nap, even if the dog doesn't need brushing.

- ☐ Start with a short session and work up to longer ones.

- ☐ Use a brush that will not hurt the dog.

Brushing tips for groomers:

- ☐ Prior to brushing, inspect the dog's skin. If the dog has a skin inflammation, or previous injury that is not completely healed, your brushing may cause pain and the dog might bite you to tell you to stop.

- ☐ Use the right brush for the right coat. Using the wrong brush may cause pain.

- ☐ Brush the dog when it is wet.

- ☐ Be patient. Rushing will cause unnecessary pain and prevent you from reading the dog's body language, especially if it is thinking about biting you.

- ☐ If appropriate, inform the owner that he needs to work on brushing at home so it will be less stressful during professional grooming.

Bathing the dog:

Bathing can be used to bond with the dog because it involves a lot of rubbing and massaging. If your tub for bathing is slippery make sure you place a towel on the bottom. If your dog panics in the tub, try feeding it there or giving it treats as a reward for getting into the tub. Using a hand-held shower head may work better than just immersing the dog in a tub of water.

Owner's responsibility for bathing:

- ☐ Ideally put the dog in a tub and use a hand-held sprayer.
- ☐ If you don't have a sprayer, fill the tub to the dog's chest level with warm water to relax it. Whichever method you use, gradually get the dog used to being bathed.
- ☐ Don't try to wet the head; dogs panic when their faces and ears get wet.
- ☐ Don't wait until the dog is dirty to give it a bath.
- ☐ At first, just put it in the tub and rinse it off to get it used to bathing.
- ☐ Do not use human shampoo; this dries out the dog's skin too much.

Blow-drying the dog:

Most dogs have two coats: an undercoat and the outside coat. Towel drying will not dry both coats entirely. Use a dog blow-dryer, which has more blowing power than a human one but doesn't get as hot. The blower will penetrate the undercoat and remove loose hair. This assures that the dog is completely dry and ready for a haircut. If a dog has a hard time with blow-drying (some dogs will attack the blower), the groomer should inform the owner and suggest he get the dog used to blow-drying at home.

Owner's responsibility for dogs that resist blow-drying:

- ☐ Gradually get your dog used to the blow-dryer by turning it on low and getting closer every day until you are close enough to blow the dog dry. Start from the other side of the room and gradually move closer.
- ☐ Don't blow the dog's face and ears.
- ☐ Blow dry from the back of the dog.

Using pacifiers for grooming aggressive or dominant dogs:

A pacifier is a toy the dog can chew on while it's being groomed. The toy is usually a tennis ball or a strong rubber toy. It will calm the dog and keep its mouth busy. Groomers should:

- ☐ Ask the owner to bring a toy along with the dog.
- ☐ Choose a toy that absorbs pressure.
- ☐ Avoid correcting aggressive or dominant dogs.

Using treats:

Although I do not usually recommend using treats to pacify dogs, they can be very helpful in smoothing things over with some dogs. In order to get quick results, use a very tasty treat such as cooked chicken or liver, not the normal dry biscuit.

How to understand a dog's body language:

Study the body language of dogs you encounter during work, as well as that of your own dog. What makes the dog excited? What makes it fearful? What stresses it? What does your behavior contribute to the dog's behavior? Familiarize yourself with other types of dogs with different temperaments and from different breeds. Notice especially how the different kinds of dogs look when they are experiencing various emotions ranging from excitement and joy to fear and aggressiveness. Before long you will begin anticipating a particular dog's behaviors just by the way it looks, and you will be able to do this for the other types of dogs you have studied.

The dog's eyes are very hard to read. Because they are small, you have to get close up to study them. When the dog is afraid or ready to attack, its eyes glare, even if it is excited about biting you. When the dog is happy or excited, its eyes look soft. When the dog is sick or sad, its eyes look weak.

Below are the most common body language signs associated with the behaviors you need to know about. Once these become recognizable, you should begin to expand your knowledge by learning the mixed signals dogs give because of undesirable genetics, incorrect training and poor environment. Also, dogs' body language varies according to whether or not they have a tail or have prick or floppy ears.

Remember that the dog's body language does not lie. It does not use its body language to trap you into getting bitten. Dogs may be master manipulators when they want their way, but, to our advantage, they do not use manipulation when they intend to attack or bite.

1. Friendly or playful body language:

☐ Total body moving side to side while moving forward in a relaxed way.

☐ Face relaxed while moving.

☐ Mouth opening and closing, relaxed.

☐ Bouncing off the ground with body swinging.

☐ Front legs stretched out forward with rear end in the air (dog appears to be bowing).

Friendly

☐ Moving forward then stopping, while bouncing from side to side.

2. Potentially threatening body language:

☐ Dog's head turned but still looking at you.

☐ Dog circling you.

☐ Head carried high or low — high head shows a dominant dog; low head shows a fearful dog.

☐ Could be barking or silent; it does not matter which.

☐ Mouth tensed when closed with lips pulled back tight — could be growling.

Potentially threatening

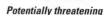

3. Dangerous body language:

☐ A surge of adrenaline will surface, and the dog's body will stiffen. The stiffness will happen whether the dog is moving or still.

☐ Hackles (hair along the neck and spine) will rise.

☐ Teeth could be showing. Dogs with extra muzzle skin that hangs down will seldom show teeth because they are unable to lift the muzzle skin.

☐ Dog maintains direct eye contact that results in tunnel vision. The dog doesn't get distracted by any other movement around it and is unable to hear its owner's commands.

☐ Dog is barking and not moving, trying to warn you to stay away.

Dangerous

☐ The dog's tail could be wagging because it is happy and excited about biting you. A dog with its tail tucked under may bite you out of fear.

☐ The dog makes a fast, direct approach then stops; its next approach may be to bite you. *Good time to utilize dog repellent spray or high-pitched sound devices.*

PERSONNEL AT ANIMAL SHELTERS, HUMANE SOCIETIES, BOARDING KENNELS AND ADOPTION FACILITIES

The shock of being caught by a stranger, put in a truck, taken into a building where many dogs are barking and then put in a small kennel or cage creates a level of stress and anxiety that is very high. The dog's true temperament becomes submerged. Just because a dog is aggressive under stress doesn't mean it's aggressive all the time. Even if the aggressiveness is temporary, however, you will still have to take precautions against getting bitten. But also understand that this may be someone's lost pet or become an adopted dog. What you do to the dog will affect its ability to be adopted in the future.

How to avoid the seven deadly sins of dog treatment:

- Don't assume the dog is friendly. A dog's behavior can change suddenly and without any warning. All dogs, regardless of age or breed, are unpredictable under stress, and even cute dogs will bite.

- Don't go down to the dog's level. This slows down your reaction time if the dog becomes aggressive.

- Stand an arm's length away; do not stand directly over the dog.

- Don't lean your face over the dog. You may get bitten in the face.

- Don't move quickly. Move slowly but don't stop moving. If you stop, you will give the dog the idea that you are afraid. When you move slowly, you are also ready to pull back if the dog becomes aggressive.

- Never lose sight of the dog.

- Never turn your back on the dog. The dog may already be afraid. If you turn away or run, the dog's instinct will tell it to chase you and bite you out of its own fear. Such a dog is a fear-biter.

Vehicles entering the dog owner's yard:

Dogs have learned that a vehicle entering their property signals someone is approaching the house. A dog will hear or see the intruder and begin barking, challenging the person and warning him to stay away. The dog often continues barking until the person gets in his vehicle and drives away. When this happens, the dog believes it has done its job by scaring the intruder away. It has won its challenge.

This barking ritual can build an adrenaline high that could make the dog break through a window or door and at worst trigger a bite if the dog gets loose. You will need to be ready to defend yourself against such a dog if this happens. See below for the sections on defensive tactics for dog encounters and attacks.

If a dog continues to bark wildly whenever you drive up, notify the owner of the danger that could result should the dog get loose. If the owner fails to take reasonable measures, such as securing the dog away from windows and doors, and making sure the dog is not loose when you arrive, refuse to come to the house.

Why dogs bark at doorbell rings and knocks at the door:

The dog has learned that the doorbell or a knock at the door means someone is on the other side. The dog will bark either because the person is invading its territory or because it is excited about meeting the person. Either way, the dog begins to associate the doorbell or knock with someone arriving. If the dog barks to protect its territory, it will believe it has won once the person leaves, making the dog confident that its bark has scared away the invader. The next time someone knocks or rings the doorbell, the dog will bark more intensely. If the person enters the house, the dog may either continue feeling aggressive about the invader or switch to being friendly because the new person gives it positive at-tention, touches it and makes friends with it.

If the dog has been barking out of excitement, it learns that when the person comes in, it will be rewarded with a touch and attention. This will make the dog bark more intensely the next time because it gets excited about the idea that the person will enter and give it friendly attention.

Caged or kenneled dog:

Before approaching a caged dog, become familiar with what its body language can tell you. See the last section of this chapter, "How to understand a dog's body language." Also, practice your own non-threatening body language as described in the "Introduction." If the dog is aggressive in the cage or kennel, try using a toy such as a tennis ball to see if the dog will play with it. Play can distract it and direct its energy away from being aggressive.

In approaching a caged or kenneled dog:

☐ Evaluate its body language. For how to do that, see the final section in this chapter.

☐ Understand that, no matter what you do, there may be some dogs you can't make friends with.

☐ Know your own limitations and level of experience. If you don't feel confident about handling a particular dog, don't set yourself up to fail. Have someone with more confidence and experience teach you how to manage the dog. If no such person is available, wait until there is one.

☐ If the dog is large or is a breed that could become dangerous and out of control, don't take it out. Wait for someone with more experience to help you.

☐ Take deep breaths to calm yourself. Dogs will sense your tension and fear.

☐ Talk calmly.

☐ Give the dog time to calm down.

☐ The dog already feels cornered, so be careful reaching into the cage.

☐ If the dog is pushed back in the corner, use a hat or something (other than your hand) to touch it to check if it will bite out of fear.

☐ Avoid using rolled-up newspaper, which may have been used as a punishment in the past.

☐ Don't spend time trying to gain the dog's confidence while it is in the cage. Dogs feel cornered when they are in a cage; so remove the dog from the cage and work on establishing trust out in the open.

Removing the dog from a kennel or cage:

- ☐ Don't hesitate when placing a slip lead on the dog.
- ☐ If the dog resists, distract it by having a second person with a treat to help secure the slip lead.
- ☐ Put on the slip lead while the dog is eating the treat.
- ☐ The dog may have never been on a leash, so expect some protesting.
- ☐ Remain still if the dog fights against the leash.
- ☐ If the dog is dangerous, use a snare and/or a three-foot square piece of quarter-inch plywood with an oval handhold (edges smoothed) cut in the top. With this you can protect your legs while pushing the dog back. Use the snare and plywood together or individually, depending on what best suits the case.

Using the snare (sometimes called control pole or rabies stick):

A snare is a pole with a noose at one end that is used to restrain loose or dangerous dogs safely. When tightened, it applies even pressure around the dog's neck so the dog doesn't injure itself or others. The snare's pole usually has a plastic coating next to the noose so the dog can bite it without injuring its teeth. However, using a snare may make some dogs respond by becoming instantly aggressive and fighting you. If this happens, remain still until the dog stops fighting. For a full discussion of what arouses aggressive dogs and how to handle them, see the chapter for "Parents," the sections on what makes dogs aggressive and how to handle aggressive dogs.

When using the snare:

Inspect the snare regularly — depending on how much you use it, you may need to replace the noose fairly often.

- ☐ Before using the snare, loosen the noose so it hangs free.
- ☐ Keep the snare at your side and down — don't hold it high or behind you. Holding it high may make it look like a weapon, and keeping it behind you may surprise the dog when you present it.
- ☐ Use both hands on the pole when putting the noose around the dog's neck and apply firm tension.

- [ ] Don't try to lift the dog with the snare pole; you could injure its neck.
- [ ] For large or strong dogs have a second person push the dog forward with the plywood board, while you handle the snare in front with two hands and move the dog into the cage or kennel.
- [ ] Never pull or jerk on the pole to get the dog to move. Step behind the dog, and it will usually walk away from you, thus walking forward.
- [ ] If the dog still refuses to move, use a three-foot square piece of plywood to push the dog forward. Walk next to or behind the dog.
- [ ] If the dog fights, remain still and allow it to fight itself.
- [ ] If you are alone with a large or strong dog, keep two hands on the pole while leading the dog into the kennel or cage.
- [ ] Once the dog is in the kennel or cage, place your foot on the door while pressing the door against the pole to prevent the dog from escaping. When removing snare from the dog, use one hand to loosen and remove it, pull the snare quickly out of the door and with the other hand lock the cage door.
- [ ] If you are putting a strange dog into your truck or van, lay down a plank for the dog to walk on in order to get into the vehicle.

Tranquilizers:

Dogs that normally would not bite are at higher risk to bite while tranquilized. The tranquilizer relaxes the dog's motor functions and causes disorganized thinking, making it unpredictable. When tranquilized, the dog appears to be drunk and is not thinking or behaving normally.

Fighting back an attack using striking techniques:

During an attack or if an attack is imminent, you may decide to use striking techniques. Your objective is to destroy the dog's confidence by striking it with dramatic, instant, painful strikes and to survive the encounter with the least amount of injury to yourself. If you think you can't strike the dog effectively, don't use this option. The dog may view your ineffective strikes as a challenge, which will make it fight even harder, thus increasing your chance of injury.

| *Kick or knee to the chest* | *Punch back of the neck where the shoulders meet* | *Punch downward with forearm to the spine* | *Uppercut to the throat* |

How to use striking techniques:

☐ Your objective is to destroy the dog's confidence and survive the encounter with the least amount of injury to yourself.

☐ Use dog repellent spray. For how to use the spray see the next section.

☐ Knee or kick the dog in the chest; this will knock the wind out of it.

☐ If possible get the dog's attention by moving something over your head; this will focus the dog's attention on the moving target and expose its chest.

☐ With your arm, punch, chop or strike the back of the neck where the shoulders meet (withers), or aim for the spine.

☐ Use your hand to punch downward between the dog's shoulder blades.

☐ Use your forearm to chop downward on the dog's spine or drive downward with your body weight going to the ground.

☐ Give an upper cut to the throat.

☐ Slam the dog to the ground or up against a wall.

☐ Keep an eye on the dog at all times.

☐ If the dog retreats, walk backwards to an escape route.

How to use dog repellent spray:

Whatever brand or type of dog repellent spray you decide to use, read the directions carefully. Check the can regularly to make sure it's still in working order. Do this by shaking the contents vigorously and spraying a small amount. Don't spray too much because repeated testing will use up the spray and leave you with too little when you really need it. If it is cold, make sure the brand you use doesn't freeze. Keep it warm by putting it next to your body.

Dog repellent spray is a nonlethal product that temporarily disorients the dog by surprising it. Dogs don't expect you to reach out and touch them without using your hands. The spray also gives the dog a quick liquid sting and causes temporary eye and nose irritation which distracts it. When it feels the irritation, it will attempt to rub off the substance by pawing at it or rolling on the ground. If you spray the repellent in the dog's mouth, it will immediately begin salivating and be distracted from biting. If the wind is low and the repellent's pressure is at full strength, most sprays can reach up to 12 feet.

In my experience, dog repellent spray works on dogs that have not decided to bite but may do so at any time, such as dogs that are circling you or barking at you but not moving. Don't think the spray is your main line of defense. Dogs that are attacking or are intent on biting you may see it as a threat or a challenge, and in their desire to overcome this challenge will become more aggressive. Such dogs are full of adrenaline and may not feel the effects of the spray. When using dog repellent spray:

☐ Remember that although you have been told to spray the dog's eyes, that is an almost impossible target to hit. Compared to humans' eyes, dogs have much larger tear ducts and a third eyelid. These assist them in recovering faster. I have been more successful spraying the dog in the mouth. This stimulates the dog's licking reflex, thus stopping it from biting. Also, the mouth is a much larger target.

☐ If the dog is biting you or has its face very close to you, try spraying into its nostrils. This will instantly cause maximum irritation, and the dog will back off.

☐ Spray in a figure eight motion, creating a continuous wall of spray. This will give you a greater chance of hitting some part of the dog's face.

☐ Start spraying as soon as you see the dog coming at you, assuming you have the can out and are ready to use it. You must be ready, because a delay will allow the dog to get too close to you or actually begin biting you.

☐ Walk backwards keeping an eye on the dog. This creates space and gives you time to think about your other options. See below for how to use striking techniques.

☐ Give verbal obedience commands to the dog ("sit," "down" or "stay") as you are walking backwards.

☐ While walking backwards, you are also escaping. Some dogs think they have done their jobs when you have gone away from their territory.

Using treats:

Although I do not usually recommend using treats to pacify dogs, for shelter and humane society workers, they can be very helpful in smoothing things over with some dogs. In order to get quick results, use a very tasty treat such as cooked chicken or liver, not the normal dry biscuit.

How to understand a dog's body language:

Study the body language of dogs you encounter during work, as well as your own pets. What makes a dog excited? What makes it fearful? What stresses it? What does your behavior contribute to the dog's behavior? Familiarize yourself with other types of dogs with different temperaments and from different breeds. Notice especially how the different kinds of dogs look when they are experiencing various emotions ranging from excitement and joy to fear and aggressiveness. Before long you will begin anticipating a particular dog's behaviors just by the way it looks, and you will be able to do this for the other types of dogs you have studied.

The dog's eyes are very hard to read. Because they are small, you have to get close up to study them. When the dog is afraid or ready to attack, its eyes glare, even if it is excited about biting you. When the dog is happy or excited in a friendly way, its eyes look soft. When the dog is sick or sad, its eyes look weak.

Below are the most common body language signs associated with the behaviors you need to know about. Once these become recognizable, you should begin to expand your knowledge by learning the mixed signals dogs give because of undesirable genetics, incorrect training and poor environment. Also, dogs' body language varies according to whether or not they have a tail or have prick or floppy ears.

Remember that the dog's body language does not lie. It does not use its body language to trap you into getting bitten. Dogs may be master manipulators when they want their way, but, to our advantage, they do not use manipulation when they intend to attack or bite.

1. Friendly or playful body language:

- ☐ Total body is moving side to side while moving forward in a relaxed way.

- ☐ Face is relaxed while dog is moving.

- ☐ Mouth is opening and closing, relaxed.

- ☐ Dog is bouncing off the ground with body swinging.

Friendly

- ☐ Front legs are stretched out forward with rear end in the air so that the dog appears to be bowing with its whole body wiggling.

- ☐ Dog is moving forward then stopping, while bouncing from side to side.

2. Potentially threatening body language:

- ☐ Dog's head is turned but the dog is still looking at you.

- ☐ Dog is circling you, attempting to attack from behind. *Good time to utilize dog repellent spray or high-pitched sound devices.*

- ☐ Head is carried high or low — high head shows a dominant dog; low head shows a fearful dog.

Potentially threatening

- ☐ Could be barking or silent; it does not matter which.

- ☐ Mouth is tensed when closed with lips curled tight — could be growling.

- ☐ Front legs are stretched out forward with rear end in the air so that the dog appears to be bowing, *but its body is stiff, not moving.*

3. Dangerous body language:

- ☐ A surge of adrenaline will surface, and the dog's body will stiffen. The stiffness will happen whether the dog is moving or still.

- ☐ Hackles (hair along the neck and spine) will rise.

- ☐ Teeth could be showing. Dogs with large muzzle skin will seldom show teeth because they are unable to lift the muzzle skin.

☐ Dog maintains direct eye contact that results in tunnel vision. The dog doesn't get distracted by any other movement around it and is unable to hear its owner's commands.

☐ Dog is barking and not moving, trying to warn you to stay away.

☐ Even if the dog's tail is wagging, it could still be planning to bite you, and it is happy and excited about the prospect. A dog with its tail tucked under may bite you out of fear.

☐ Dog makes a fast, direct approach then stops; its next approach may be to bite you. *Good time to utilize dog repellent spray or high-pitched sound devices.*

Dangerous

Keep in mind:

If the attack is imminent and you are knocked down to the ground, curl up in a protective ball. It is not instinctive for a single, domesticated dog, or dogs without a strong killing instinct, to attack its prey when its prey is motionless. This is the same concept that you may have learned about bear attacks. Usually, neither a bear nor a dog will attack a motionless person or prey. This does not hold true for dogs with a strong killing instinct, however. For a description of how they behave, see the chapter on "Dogs That Are Dangerous or Fighters."

HOME CARE VISITORS

Before visiting the home, tell the residents that, if they have a dog, you will sound your horn so they can secure the dog before you enter the house. If you haven't done this, or if the resident hasn't secured the dog and you encounter it by surprise, you will need to know the following information about dog encounters.

Any dog can be a threat. All dogs will bite when protecting themselves, their property and/or their owners. Since dogs can't talk; they may bite to tell you "No" or "Stop" — even if it's your own dog.

How can you tell the difference between a dog encounter and an attack? In a dog encounter, the dog will confront you but decide not to attack. In an attack the dog has decided to bite you. It's hard to tell when a dog encounter will turn into an attack. Sometimes you

surprise a dog and it will attack right away. Or it may first try to warn you off. You can't know what any dog will do in the face of stress, so you have to be prepared for both a harmless encounter and an actual attack when you meet a dog. You don't want to injure or kill a harmless dog, but you don't want to get bitten either. The detailed instructions and checklists that follow will help you know what is best to do in a simple encounter and an outright attack.

How to avoid the five deadly sins of dog encounters:

- Never assume all dogs are friendly. A dog's behavior can change suddenly and without any warning. Dogs under stress are unpredictable, and even cute dogs will bite.

- Never run from any dog — running triggers the dog's hunting instinct and makes it chase you.

- Never turn your back on any dog. The dog may already be afraid. If you turn away or run, the dog's instinct will tell it to chase you and bite you out of its own fear. Such a dog is a fear-biter.

- Don't depend on the owner to know how his dog will behave under stress.

- Don't stand face to face with a dog during a threat. This will only challenge the dog to a fight.

When arriving at a location check for:

- ☐ "Beware of Dog" signs

- ☐ dog house, chains, bowls

- ☐ dog feces in yard — the smell may strike you before you actually see them

- ☐ patches of dead grass where the dog's urine has killed it

- ☐ worn track around fence — an indication that the dog is out a lot

- ☐ sleeping or unalert dog — shake fence or make any noise to alert or wake up dog. If the dog is tied up and you have to cross its path, don't do so. An aggressive dog may get a burst of strength and break its rope or chain.

- ☐ If the dog is outside when you arrive, telephone the owner and ask him to secure the dog. If the owner doesn't do that, refuse to make the visit.

- ☐ If the dog is in a yard where an underground electric fence is confining it, don't consider that type of fence a valid means of containment. The dog may get a rush of adrenaline and cross the fence line. The dog's state of aggression will numb its body from the shock and it may bite you.

- ☐ Use your discretion. If your safety is at risk refuse to enter the house and reschedule the appointment.

Once in the house, if a dog is present:

☐ Evaluate the dog's body language. See section at the end of this chapter for a description of body language.

☐ Make it your policy not to have dogs around during your visit. The dog will sense if the owner is nervous. If you are drawing blood, having her perform exercises and especially if you are touching the owner, make sure the dog is secured in another part of the house or apartment.

☐ Tell the owner to place the dog in a secure area. Try saying, "It's our policy that dogs not be present during the visit." If the owner persists in keeping the dog in the room, try saying, "I would feel more comfortable if the dog were in a secure area."

☐ If the dog becomes aggressive, don't grasp the owner in an attempt to use her as a shield. The dog may view your actions as an attack on the owner and may bite you to protect her.

Vehicles entering the dog owner's yard:

Dogs have learned that a vehicle entering their property signals someone approaching the house. A dog will hear or see the intruder and begin barking, challenging the person and warning him to stay away. The dog often continues barking until the person gets in his vehicle and drives away. When this happens, the dog believes it has done its job by scaring the intruder away. It has won its challenge.

This barking ritual can build an adrenaline high that could make the dog break through a window or door and at worst trigger a bite if the dog gets loose. You will need to be ready to defend yourself against such a dog if this happens. See below for the sections on defensive tactics for dog encounters and attacks.

If a dog continues to bark wildly whenever you drive up, notify the owner of the danger that could result should the dog get loose. If the owner fails to take reasonable measures, such as securing the dog away from windows and doors and making sure the dog is not loose when you arrive, refuse to come to the house.

Why dogs bark at doorbell rings and knocks at the door:

The dog has learned that the doorbell or a knock at the door means someone is on the other side. The dog will bark either because the person is invading its territory or because it is excited about meeting the person. Either way, the dog begins to associate the doorbell or knock with someone arriving. If the dog barks to protect its territory, it will believe it has won once the person leaves, making the dog confident that its bark has scared away the invader. The next time someone knocks or rings the doorbell, the dog will bark more intensely. If the person enters the house, the dog may either continue feeling aggressive about the invader or switch to being friendly because the new person gives it positive attention, touches it and makes friends with it.

If the dog has been barking out of excitement, it learns that when the person comes in, it will be rewarded with a touch and attention. This will make the dog bark more intensely the next time because it gets excited about the idea that the person will enter and give it friendly attention.

When giving something to a person with a dog or taking anything from him:

☐ Have the person come to you; this will make the dog invade your space instead of you invading its personal space. A dog may bite you if you invade its space or may perceive your coming towards it as a threat.

☐ Have the person take the object while you hold the object close to you; the dog could perceive your hand reaching out as a threat.

☐ When leaving, do not turn your back on the dog and walk away. Instead, either walk slowly backwards to a safe distance while always keeping your eye on the dog or allow the owner and dog to leave first.

☐ If the dog becomes aggressive at any time, walk backwards to create space and place the object you are trying to give the person somewhere else. Tell the owner to stop coming towards you.

☐ If a screened door is the only door between you and the dog, and the dog is jumping on it, place your foot and hand on the door to make sure the dog doesn't force it open. If the door is broken, shout for owner and/or spray the dog with repellent through screen. See below for a discussion of how to use dog repellent spray.

Defensive tactics against a dog encounter:

☐ Do not run; you will only cause the dog's biting instinct to surface.

☐ If a dog is following you, stop and evaluate. The dog may just want to smell you.

☐ Stop and stand sideways, so the dog doesn't think you are challenging it.

☐ Avoid quick movement. The dog could be nervous and a quick movement may trigger fear-biting.

☐ If the dog is coming towards you, move backwards and sideways, keeping an eye on the dog. This gives you space and time to react.

☐ Carry a high-pitched sound device. See below for how to use the device.

☐ Give it some common commands ("stay," "sit," "down"). This makes the dog think maybe you are in charge.

☐ Be careful about giving negative commands ("no," "get out of here"). They may work, but if a dog perceives them as a threat you may escalate the dog's aggression and get bitten.

☐ Look at the dog, but don't stare into its eyes. Look at the top of its head or at its eyebrows. Looking away may tell the dog it has won the challenge, and it may bite you.

☐ If you know the dog, relax it by using its name.

☐ Once the dog loses interest in you, move slowly backwards until you are out of its sight.

☐ Provide the dog room for an escape by not cutting off escape routes such as a door or gate.

☐ Remain calm by taking deep breaths. This will calm your body; dogs can sense tension and fear. If the dog senses your fear (and it probably will), it will gain confidence about biting you.

Defending yourself against a dog attack: stop, drop and curl:

If the attack is imminent, fall to the ground and curl up in a ball, protecting your stomach, face and ears. Do not scream or yell, this will only make the dog more confident. Its survival instinct will surface, and it will attack you with renewed force. Once on the ground, you are no longer a threat. Listen to what the dog is doing. Try to keep an eye on the dog while standing up slowly.

How to defend yourself if an attack is threatened but not imminent:

☐ Stop stand sideways, so the dog doesn't think you are challenging it.

☐ Evaluate the dog's body language. See "How to understand a dog's body language" at the end of this section.

☐ If the dog is attacking, present a moving target by waving something in front of the dog. Walk or run backwards, keeping an eye on the dog.

Don't run or turn your back.

☐ If bitten *don't pull away.* This is very difficult to do, but if you pull away, the bite will be much more serious because the dog will resist having anything pulled from its mouth and will fight harder to hold on, causing more skin-tearing and deeper wounds.

☐ Use defensive options in escalating order: verbal commands, dog repellent spray, striking techniques.

☐ As soon as you can, notify Animal Control or the police.

How to use dog repellent spray:

Whatever brand or type of dog repellent spray you decide to use, read the directions carefully. Check the can regularly to make sure it's still in working order. Do this by shaking the contents vigorously and spraying a small amount. Don't spray too much because repeated testing will use up the spray and leave you with too little when you really need it. If it is cold, make sure the brand you use doesn't freeze. Keep it warm by putting it next to your body.

Dog repellent spray is a nonlethal product that temporarily disorients the dog by surprising it. Dogs don't expect you to reach out and touch them without using your hands. The spray also gives the dog a quick liquid sting and causes temporary eye and nose irritation which distracts it. When it feels the irritation, it will attempt to rub off the substance by pawing at it or rolling on the ground. If you spray the repellent in the dog's mouth, it will immediately begin salivating and be distracted from biting. If the wind is low and the repellent's pressure is at full strength, most sprays can reach up to 12 feet.

In my experience, the spray works on dogs that have not decided to bite but may do so at any time, such as dogs that are circling you or barking at you but not moving. Don't think the spray is your main line of defense. Dogs that are attacking or are intent on biting you may see it as a threat or a challenge, and in their desire to overcome this challenge will become more aggressive. Such dogs are full of adrenaline and may not feel the spray's effects. When using dog repellent spray:

☐ Remember that although you have been told to spray the dog's eyes, that is an almost impossible target to hit. Compared to humans' eyes, dogs have much larger tear ducts and a third eyelid. These assist them in recovering faster. I have been more successful spraying the dog in the mouth. This stimulates the dog's licking reflex, thus stopping it from biting. Also, the mouth is a much larger target.

☐ If the dog is biting you or has its face very close to you, try spraying into its nostrils. This will instantly cause maximum irritation, and the dog will back off.

☐ Spray in a figure eight motion, creating a continuous wall of spray. This will give you a greater chance of hitting some part of the dog's face.

- [ ] Start spraying as soon as you see the dog coming at you, assuming you have the can out and are ready to use it. You must be ready, because a delay will allow the dog to get too close to you or actually begin biting you.

- [ ] Walk slowly backwards keeping an eye on the dog. This creates space and gives you time to think about your other options. See below for how to use striking techniques.

- [ ] Give verbal obedience commands to the dog ("sit," "down" or "stay") as you are walking backwards.

- [ ] While walking backwards, you are also escaping. Some dogs think they have done their jobs when you have gone away from their territory.

High-pitched sound devices:

These emit a high-pitched tone that humans can't hear but dogs can. The device should be used as soon as the dog encounter becomes threatening. These devices cause discomfort to the dog's hearing but have no negative aftereffects. They are about the size of a garage-door opener and fit in the palm of your hand or clip onto your waistband or belt. When you push the activating button, the dog first becomes surprised because it can't tell where the high-pitched sound is coming from. Then it quickly realizes that as it gets closer to you, the sound gets more intense. Being surprised and disturbed by the sound, the dog may not come any closer to you. This device doesn't work on all dogs, but it is an effective protection against dogs that have not yet decided to bite you but could do so at any moment.

Fighting back an attack using striking techniques:

During an attack or if an attack is imminent, you may decide to use striking techniques. Your objective is to destroy the dog's confidence by striking it with dramatic, instant, painful strikes and to survive the encounter with the least amount of injury to yourself. If you think you can't strike the dog effectively, don't use this option. The dog may view your ineffective strikes as a challenge, which will make it fight even harder, thus increasing your chance of injury.

Kick or knee to the chest

Punch back of the neck where the shoulders meet

Punch downward with forearm to the spine

Uppercut to the throat

How to use striking techniques:

- ☐ Knee or kick the dog in the chest; this will knock the wind out of it.
- ☐ If possible get the dog's attention by moving something over your head; this will get the dog to focus on the moving target and expose its chest.
- ☐ Punch, chop or strike the back of the neck where the shoulders meet, or aim for the spine. Use any object that will make an impact.
- ☐ Use your forearm to punch downward on the dog's spine or drive downward with your body weight going to the ground.
- ☐ Give an upper cut to the throat.
- ☐ Slam the dog to the ground or up against a wall.
- ☐ Keep an eye on the dog at all times.
- ☐ If the dog retreats, walk backwards to an escape route.

Loose dogs and stray dogs (notify Animal Control or the police):

When making your visit, you may encounter a loose dog or a stray dog. Such dogs have been allowed to determine their own territory. They now believe their roaming area, regardless of the size, belongs to them. This makes them unpredictable even if they appear friendly. Anyone invading their territory will make the dogs protect it, so stay away from all stray dogs, and notify Animal Control or the police.

Dogs trained for protection:

If your client has a protection dog that has not been put in a secure area, you need to be wary about encountering it. While being trained to protect its owner and her property, the dog has always been allowed to win. Because of this, the dog's confidence has been so strongly built up that it thinks it can overcome anything a human can give out. Be prepared to divert the dog's attention from you to a target object that it can defeat, such as a hat or sack. While it is attacking the object, it will become vulnerable to your repellent spray, striking techniques or stronger measures.

Dogs not trained for protection:

Similar to a dog trained for protection, a dog not specifically trained for protection will still instinctively protect its house or yard as its territory. It believes that it has won all challenges from people invading its space. After all, it scares you and others away when it barks.

Why dogs try to scare off people in uniforms:

If you are wearing a uniform, you need to know why dogs will react to you by barking. A uniformed person enters the dog's yard. It barks; the person leaves. The dog thinks that it has scared him away. Thus, uniformed people who come and go as part of their jobs have indirectly built the dog's confidence in its ability to challenge them. Now the dog perceives anyone wearing a uniform who invades its territory as a threat. This makes the dog potentially dangerous even if it appears friendly.

The treat myth:

If you carry treats to smooth things over with some dogs, the dogs will see people entering their property as a good thing. The problem arises when new home care visitors or strangers get confused by the approaching dog. The dog is looking for its treat, but the stranger may well think the dog is about to attack and will hit it, spray it with repellent, or use even stronger force. Your treats have created a painful, even lethal, trap for the dog.

How to understand a dog's body language:

Study the body language of dogs you encounter during work, as well as your own pets. What makes a dog excited? What makes it fearful? What stresses it? What does your behavior contribute to the dog's behavior? Familiarize yourself with other types of dogs with different temperaments and from different breeds. Notice especially how the different kinds of dogs look when they are experiencing various emotions ranging from excitement and joy to fear and aggressiveness. Before long you will begin anticipating a particular dog's behaviors just by the way it looks, and you will be able to do this for the other types of dogs you have studied.

The dog's eyes are very hard to read. Because they are small, you have to get close up to study them. When the dog is afraid or ready to attack, its eyes glare, even if it is excited about biting you. When the dog is happy or excited in a friendly way, its eyes look soft. When the dog is sick or sad, its eyes look weak.

Below are the most common body language signs associated with the behaviors you need to know about. Once these become recognizable, you should begin to expand your knowledge by learning the mixed signals dogs give because of undesirable genetics, incorrect training and poor environment. Also, dogs' body language varies according to whether or not they have a tail or have prick or floppy ears.

Remember that the dog's body language does not lie. It does not use its body language to trap you into getting bitten. Dogs may be master manipulators when they want their way, but, to our advantage, they do not use manipulation when they intend to attack or bite.

1. Friendly or playful body language:

☐ Total body is moving side to side while moving forward in a relaxed way.

☐ Face is relaxed while dog is moving.

☐ Mouth is opening and closing, relaxed.

☐ Dog is bouncing off the ground with body swinging.

☐ Front legs are stretched out forward with rear end in the air so that the dog appears to be bowing with its whole body wiggling.

☐ Dog is moving forward then stopping, while bouncing from side to side.

Friendly

2. Potentially threatening body language:

☐ Dog's head is turned but the dog is still looking at you.

☐ Dog is circling you, attempting to attack from be- hind. *Good time to utilize dog repellent spray or high-pitched sound devices.*

☐ Head is carried high or low — high head shows a dominant dog; low head shows a fearful dog.

☐ Could be barking or silent; it does not matter which.

Potentially threatening

☐ Mouth is tensed when closed with lips curled tight — could be growling.

☐ Front legs are stretched out forward with rear end in the air so that the dog appears to be bowing, *but its body is stiff, not moving.*

3. Dangerous body language:

☐ A surge of adrenaline will surface, and the dog's body will stiffen. The stiffness will happen whether the dog is moving or still.

☐ Hackles (hair along the neck and spine) will rise.

☐ Teeth could be showing. Dogs with large muzzle skin will seldom show teeth be- cause they are unable to lift the muzzle skin.

☐ Dog maintains direct eye contact that results in tunnel vision. The dog doesn't get distracted by any other movement around it and is unable to hear its owner's commands.

☐ Dog is barking and not moving, trying to warn you to stay away.

☐ The dog's tail could be wagging because it is happy and excited about biting you. A dog with its tail tucked under may bite you out of fear.

Dangerous

☐ The dog makes a fast, direct approach then stops; its next approach may be to bite you. *Good time to uti- lize dog repellent spray or high-pitched sound devices.*

Keep in mind:

If the attack is imminent and you are knocked down to the ground, curl up in a protective ball. It is not instinctive for a single, domesticated dog, or dogs without a strong killing in- stinct, to attack its prey when its prey is motionless. This is the same concept that you may have learned about bear attacks. Usually, neither a bear nor a dog will attack a motionless person or prey. This does not hold true for dogs with a strong killing instinct, however. For a description of how they behave, see the chapter on "Dogs That Are Dangerous or Fighters, Because of Breeding or Learned Behavior."

PREPARING YOURSELF
FOR DOG ENCOUNTERS FOR:

LAW ENFORCEMENT OFFICERS

Any dog can be a threat. All dogs will bite when protecting themselves, their property, and/or their owners. Since dogs can't talk, they may bite to tell you "No" or "Stop."

How can you tell the difference between a dog encounter and an attack? In a dog encounter, the dog will confront you but decide not to attack. In an attack the dog has decided to bite you. It's hard to tell when a dog encounter will turn into an attack. Sometimes you surprise a dog and it will attack right away, or it may first try to warn you off. You can't know what any dog will do in the face of stress, so you have to be prepared for both a harmless encounter and an actual attack when you meet a dog. You don't want to injure or kill a harmless dog, but you don't want to get bitten either. The detailed instructions and checklists that follow will help you know what is best to do in a simple encounter and an outright attack.

How to avoid the five deadly sins of dog encounters:

- ➥ Never assume all dogs are friendly. A dog's behavior can change suddenly and without warning. Dogs under stress are unpredictable, and even cute dogs will bite.

- ➥ Never run from any dog — running triggers the dog's hunting instinct and makes it chase you.

- ➥ Never turn your back on any dog. The dog may already be afraid. If you turn away or run, the dog's instinct will tell it to chase you and bite you out of its own fear. Such a dog is a fear-biter.

- ➥ Don't depend on the owner to know how his dog will behave under stress.

- ➥ Don't stand face to face with a dog during a threat. This will only challenge the dog to a fight.

When arriving at a location check for:

- ☐ "Beware of Dog" signs
- ☐ dog house, chains, bowls
- ☐ dog feces in yard — the smell may strike you before you actually see them
- ☐ patches of dead grass where the dog's urine has killed it
- ☐ worn track around fence — an indication that the dog is out a lot
- ☐ sleeping or unalert dog — shake fence or make any noise to alert or wake up dog.
- ☐ If the dog is tied up and you have to cross its path, be cautious and ready to protect yourself, because an aggressive dog may get a burst of strength and break its rope or chain.
- ☐ If the dog is in a yard where an underground electric fence is confining it don't consider that type of fence a valid means of containment. The dog may get a rush of adrenaline and cross the fence line. The dog's state of aggression will numb its body from the shock and it may bite you.

The treat myth:

If you carry treats to smooth things over with some dogs, the dogs will see people entering their property as a good thing. The problem arises when a new police officer comes on the property, and the dog runs toward him looking for a treat. The officer may think the dog is about to attack and may hit it, spray it with dog repellent it or even shoot it. Your treats have created a painful, even lethal, trap for the dog.

Vehicles entering the dog owner's yard:

Dogs have learned that a vehicle entering their property signals someone approaching the house. A dog will hear or see the intruder and begin barking, challenging the person and warning him to stay away. The dog often continues barking until the person gets in his vehicle and drives away. When this happens, the dog believes it has done its job by scaring the intruder away. It has won its challenge.

This barking ritual can build an adrenaline high that could make the dog break through a window or door and at worst trigger a bite if the dog gets loose. You will need to be ready to defend yourself against such a dog if this happen. See below for the sections on defensive tactics for dog encounters and attacks.

Why dogs bark at doorbell rings and knocks at the door:

The dog has learned that the doorbell or a knock at the door means someone is on the other side. The dog will bark either because the person is invading its territory or because it is excited about meeting the person. Either way, the dog begins to associate the doorbell or knock with someone arriving. If the dog barks to protect its territory, it will believe it has won once the person leaves, making the dog confident that its bark has scared away the invader. The next time someone knocks or rings the doorbell, the dog will bark more intensely. If the person enters the house, the dog may either continue feeling aggressive about the invader or switch to being friendly because the new person gives it positive attention, touches it and makes friends with it.

If the dog has been barking out of excitement, it learns that when the person comes in, it will be rewarded with a touch and attention. This will make the dog bark more intensely the next time because it gets excited about the idea that the person will enter and give it friendly attention.

Why dogs try to scare off people in uniforms:

If you are wearing a uniform, you need to know why dogs will react to you by barking. A uniformed person enters the dog's yard. It barks; the person leaves. The dog thinks that it has scared the person away. Thus, uniformed people who come and go as part of their jobs have indirectly built the dog's confidence in its ability to challenge them. Now the dog perceives anyone wearing a uniform who invades its territory as a threat. This makes the dog potentially dangerous even if it appears friendly.

If owner is present:

- ☐ Insist the dog be placed in a secure area. Try saying, "I *need* you to put the dog away." If the owner resists, you could try saying, "I would feel better if you would put your dog away."

- ☐ Never pet the dog. You are not part of the dog's social order, and it may bite you even if you have petted it before.

- ☐ Avoid quick movements. The dog could be nervous, and a quick movement will trigger its fear-biting response.

- ☐ If the owner answers the door with the dog or the dog shows up during the meeting and becomes aggressive, prevent the dog from escaping and biting by grasping the door and closing it. If the dog is used as a distraction, if time permits utilize your options: verbal commands, dog repellent spray, striking techniques or deadly force and keep an eye on the person.

When giving something to a person with a dog or taking anything from him:

- ☐ Have the person come to you; this will make the dog invade your space instead of you invading its personal space. A dog may bite you if you invade its space or may perceive your coming towards it as a threat.

- ☐ Have the person take the object while you hold the object close to you; the dog could perceive your hand reaching out as a threat.

- ☐ When leaving, do not turn your back on the dog and walk away. Instead, either walk slowly backwards to a safe distance while always keeping your eye on the dog or allow the owner and dog to leave first.

- ☐ If the dog becomes aggressive at any time, walk backwards to create space and place the object you are trying to give the person somewhere else. Tell the owner to stop coming towards you.

- ☐ If a screened door is the only door between you and the dog and the dog is jumping on it, place your foot and hand on the door to make sure the dog doesn't force it open. If the door is broken, shout for the owner and/or spray repellent at the dog through screen. See below for a discussion of how to use dog repellent spray.

Loose dogs and stray dogs:

A loose dog or a stray dog has been allowed to determine its own territory. The dog now believes its roaming area, regardless of the size, belongs to it. This makes the dog unpredictable even if it appears friendly. Anyone invading its territory will make the dog protect it, so take full safety precautions when approaching one.

Dogs trained for protection:

While being trained to protect its owner and her property, the dog has always been allowed to win. Because of this, the dog's confidence has been so strongly built up that it thinks it can overcome anything a human can give out. Be prepared to divert the dog's attention from you to a target object that it can defeat, such as a hat or sack. While it is attacking the object, it will become vulnerable to your repellent spray, taser, striking techniques or stronger measures, including lethal force.

Dogs not trained for protection:

Similar to a dog trained for protection, a dog not specifically trained for protection will still instinctively protect its house or yard as its territory. It believes that it has won all challenges from people invading its space. After all, it scares you and others away when it barks.

Be careful jumping fences during foot chases:

- [ ] Shake fence to alert or wake up dog.
- [ ] Be aware that during a foot chase, the suspect may alert the dog by running past it or jumping over fence, leaving you to deal with an aroused dog.

Defensive tactics against a dog encounter:

- [ ] Do not run; you will only cause the dog's biting instinct to surface. Avoid quick movement. The dog could be nervous, and a quick movement may trigger fear-biting.
- [ ] Stand sideways, gun side away from the dog.
- [ ] Give it some common commands ("stay," "sit," "down"). This makes the dog think maybe you are in charge.
- [ ] Be careful about giving negative commands ("no," "get out of here"). They may work, but if a dog perceives them as a threat, you may escalate the dog's aggression.
- [ ] If the dog is coming towards you, move backwards and sideways, keeping your eye on the dog. This gives you space and time to react.
- [ ] Look at the dog, but don't stare into its eyes. Look at the top of its head or at its eyebrows. Looking away may tell the dog it has won the challenge, and it may bite you.
- [ ] Once the dog loses interest in you, move slowly backwards until you are out of its sight.
- [ ] Provide the dog room for an escape by not cutting off escape routes such as a door or gate.
- [ ] Remain calm by taking deep breaths. This will calm your body; dogs can sense tension and fear. If the dog senses your fear (and it probably will), it will gain confidence about biting you.

Defending yourself against a dog attack

- [ ] Stop stand sideways, gun side away. If you face the dog, it will think you are challenging it.
- [ ] Evaluate the dog's body language. See "How to understand a dog's body language" at the end of this chapter.
- [ ] If the dog is attacking, present a moving target by waving something in front of the dog. Walk slowly backwards, keeping an eye on the dog. Then, if necessary, use lethal force against it.
- [ ] If bitten *don't pull away.* This is very difficult to do, but if you pull away, the bite will be much more serious because the dog will resist having anything pulled from its mouth and will fight harder to hold on, causing more skin-tearing and deeper wounds.
- [ ] Use defensive options in escalating order: verbal commands, dog repellent spray, taser, striking techniques, impact weapons and, as a last resort, lethal force.
- [ ] As soon as you can, notify Animal Control.

Fighting back an attack using striking techniques:

During an attack or if an attack is imminent, you may decide to use striking techniques. Your objective is to destroy the dog's confidence by striking it with dramatic, instant, painful strikes and to survive the encounter with the least amount of injury to yourself. If you think you can't strike the dog effectively, don't use this option. The dog may view your ineffective strikes as a challenge, which will make it fight even harder, thus increasing your chance of injury.

Kick or knee to the chest

Punch back of the neck where the shoulders meet

Punch downward with forearm to the spine

Uppercut to the throat

How to use striking techniques:

- ☐ Knee or kick the dog in the chest; this will knock the wind out of it.
- ☐ If possible get the dog's attention by moving something over your head; this will get the dog to focus on the moving target and expose its chest.
- ☐ Punch, chop or strike where the shoulders meet (withers), or aim for the spine. Use any device that will make an impact.
- ☐ Use your forearm to punch downward on the dog's spine or drive downward with your body weight going to the ground.
- ☐ Give an upper cut to the throat.
- ☐ Slam the dog to the ground or up against a wall.
- ☐ Keep an eye on the dog at all times.
- ☐ If the dog retreats, walk backwards to an escape route.

How to use dog repellent spray:

Whatever brand or type of dog repellent spray you decide to use, read the directions carefully. Check the can regularly to make sure it's still in working order. Do this by shaking the contents vigorously and spraying a small amount. Don't spray too much because repeated testing will use up the spray and leave you with too little when you really need it. If it is cold, make sure the brand you use doesn't freeze. Keep it warm by putting it next to your body.

Dog repellent spray is a nonlethal product that temporarily disorients the dog by surprising it. Dogs don't expect you to reach out and touch them without using your hands.

The spray also gives the dog a quick liquid sting and causes temporary eye and nose irritation which distracts it. When it feels the irritation, it will attempt to rub off the substance by pawing at it or rolling on the ground. If you spray the repellent in the dog's mouth, it will immediately begin salivating and be distracted from biting. If the wind is low and the repellent's pressure is at full strength, most sprays can reach up to 12 feet.

In my experience, dog repellent spray works on dogs that have not decided to bite but may do so at any time, such as dogs that are circling you, or barking at you but not moving. Don't think the spray is your main line of defense. Dogs that are attacking or are intent on biting you may see it as a threat or a challenge, and in their desire to overcome this challenge will become more aggressive. Such dogs are full of adrenaline and may not feel the spray's effects. When using dog repellent spray:

- [ ] Remember that although you have been told to spray the dog's eyes, that is an almost impossible target to hit. Compared to humans' eyes, dogs have much larger tear ducts and a third eyelid. These assist them in recovering faster. I have been more successful spraying the dog in the mouth. This stimulates the dog's licking reflex, thus stopping it from biting. Also, the mouth is a much larger target.

- [ ] If the dog is biting you or has its face very close to you, try spraying into its nostrils. This will instantly cause maximum irritation, and the dog will back off.

- [ ] Spray in a figure eight motion, creating a continuous wall of spray. This will give you a greater chance of hitting some part of the dog's face.

- [ ] Start spraying as soon as you see the dog coming at you, assuming you have the can out and are ready to use it. You must be ready, because a delay will allow the dog to get too close to you or actually begin biting you.

- [ ] Walk slowly backwards, keeping an eye on the dog. This creates space and gives you time to think about your other options, such as striking techniques. See below for how to use striking techniques.

- [ ] Give verbal obedience commands to the dog ("sit," "down" or "stay") as you are walking slowly backwards.

- [ ] While walking backwards, you are also escaping. Some dogs think they have done their jobs when you have gone away from their territory.

Using a fire extinguisher against a dog attack:

☐ Disables dog temporarily.

☐ Restricts oxygen intake temporarily.

☐ Is most effective when you spray in two to three second bursts.

☐ Has little to no effect on dogs that are fighting.

☐ *But,* used indoors, it may create fog which lowers visibility or lowers the oxygen level, temporarily incapacitating you.

Gaining entry to a house with a dog inside:

☐ Have back-up officer carry a fire extinguisher. If you are alone, wait for backup.

☐ Make sure the dog has an escape route.

☐ If possible and if the backyard is fenced, have the second officer open back door to let the dog outside.

☐ If you can't let the dog out, use the second officer to distract the dog by throwing a blanket over it or pushing it into another room.

☐ Keep your eye on the dog at all times.

☐ If available, use a shield or an ambulance backboard to push the dog into another room.

☐ Use lethal force as a last resort only. The dog is doing its job by protecting its owner and property.

Gaining entry into a vehicle with a dog inside during an emergency such as a serious accident:

☐ Evaluate the dog's condition. Is it bleeding, limping, not moving? Use a backboard or shield to block the dog.

☐ If the vehicle's doors are open, allow the dog to escape.

☐ Use a shield or ambulance backboard to block or push dog out of the car.

☐ If the car doors are locked, break two windows: the first one for opening the door and the second one to give the dog an escape route.

☐ Use a second officer for a distraction to get the victim out of the vehicle.

☐ Use lethal force as a last resort only. The dog is doing its job by protecting its owner and the car. Also, your bullet could ricochet striking the person or you.

If the dog is guarding its owner while the owner is unresponsive:

The dog views anyone approaching its owner as a threat. If its owner is unresponsive, the dog may become aware of its owner's vulnerability and will become aggressive to keep you away. The dog has no idea that you are trying to assist its owner or save his life. It is only doing what comes instinctively. Some dogs will even lie right on top of their owners when they are guarding them or at least stay firmly by their side. Others will refuse to let anyone enter their yard or house. Your goal is to remove the dog without using deadly force. Here is how you can approach the dog:

- ☐ First evaluate the dog's body language. The dog may be comforting the owner, or it may be a threat to you. See the last section in this chapter, "How to understand a dog's body language."

- ☐ While approaching the dog, speak to it in a calm voice and wait for a friendly response in body language, such as a relaxed head and body.

- ☐ If the dog is friendly, you should still secure it, because the dog could switch to being aggressive at any time.

- ☐ If the dog is charging and then retreating to its owner, use a barrier such as a chair, backboard or heavy sheet to block the dog from biting you.

- ☐ Use the barrier to push the dog into a room or a secure area.

- ☐ If the dog refuses to move, throw a sheet over it, wrap the sheet around the dog and pull it into another room or secure area.

- ☐ If the above attempts fail, taser the dog, but allow it to have an area of escape, such as an open room or backyard.

- ☐ Don't use repellent spray; it may affect the unresponsive owner.

- ☐ Don't use a fire extinguisher; it may create a fog that will prevent you from seeing clearly, and its spray may remove oxygen from the air, injuring you and the unresponsive owner.

- ☐ As a last resort, exercise lethal force, always being aware of your surroundings to avoid ricochets from stray bullets and to avoid hitting anyone else.

Using a taser:

The taser is a nonlethal tool that looks like a handgun. When triggered, it launches probes that penetrate clothing or fur as much as two inches thick from up to 21 feet away. In close contact, the taser functions as a stun gun. It transmits intense electrical impulses (50,000 volts) that temporarily numb and immobilize the target.

Although the taser was not originally designed to be used on animals, it has proved effective on hostile dogs. Certain kinds of dogs have been bred to win at any cost. During an attack, their adrenaline will soar, and tunnel vision will occur. The dog will become numb to pain and other distractions such as dog repellent spray, punches and impact weapons. Tests have shown that the taser can penetrate an adrenaline

M26 vs. Pit Bull

Kicks, Baton, and OC were ineffective. Pit bull was attacking police K-9, biting the throat. M26 was deployed to prevent potential death of K-9.

rush and break up a dog's tunnel vision, making it a very useful nonlethal weapon against an attacking dog.

But the dog will recover quickly, so if time and circumstances permit, you will need a plan to ward off further attacks. With humans, we cuff them after tasering them. With a dog, we use a snare. If time permits, before tasering the dog, notify Animal Control to bring a snare. If time doesn't permit and you have no snare, then use the taser or lethal force if necessary. In using the taser:

- ☐ Aim at body mass.
- ☐ Turn the taser to a three o'clock or nine o'clock position in order to get a horizontal target picture.
- ☐ Because most attacks occur from the front, you should walk backwards and sideways for a better shot at the dog's body mass.
- ☐ Stay alert for a second attack.
- ☐ If you use the taser in a room, make sure the dog has a way out.
- ☐ As a last resort, use lethal force.

Exercising lethal force as a last resort:

- ☐ If the dog is attacking, walk slowly backwards, keeping an eye on the dog, and exercise lethal force.
- ☐ Aim at the dog's body mass. Its head is armor-plated and presents a small target, but see the next item, especially if the situation is extremely dangerous.
- ☐ If the dog's body is moving quickly back and forth and you are a good shot, aim at the head, targeting the inner part of the ear. This is a small target, but if successful, your shot will cause instant death and may prevent ricochet by trapping the bullet inside the skull.
- ☐ If the dog is directly in front of you, aim for the top center of the shoulders or hips.
- ☐ Be aware of your surroundings — use striking techniques in crowded areas, because a bullet could ricochet.

☐ Understand that the first shot might only distract the dog. You want to stop its attack, so you may have to shoot more than once.

☐ Don't assume the dog is not a threat if it has been shot. It will have an adrenaline high while attacking and may not feel pain even from a shot until it has calmed down.

☐ If time and circumstances permit, use frangible rounds to prevent a solid bullet from going straight through the dog, ricocheting and hitting someone else.

How to understand a dog's body language:

Study the body language of dogs you encounter during work, as well as your own pets. What makes the dog excited? What makes it fearful? What stresses it? What does your behavior contribute to the dog's behavior? Familiarize yourself with other types of dogs with different temperaments and from different breeds. Notice especially how the different kinds of dogs look when they are experiencing various emotions from excitement and joy to fear and aggression. Before long you will begin anticipating a particular dog's behaviors just by the way it looks, and you will be able to do this for the other types of dogs you have studied.

The dog's eyes are hard to read. They are small, and you have to get close up to study them. When the dog is afraid or ready to attack, its eyes glare, even if it is excited about biting you. When the dog is happy or excited in a friendly way, its eyes look soft. When the dog is sick or sad, its eyes look weak.

Below are the most common body language signs associated with the behaviors you need to know about. Once these become recognizable, you should begin to expand your knowledge by learning the mixed signals dogs give because of undesirable genetics, incorrect training and poor environment. Also, dogs' body language varies according to whether or not they have a tail or have prick or floppy ears.

Remember that the dog's body language does not lie. It does not use its body language to trap you into getting bitten. Dogs may be master manipulators when they want their way, but, to our advantage, they do not use manipulation when they intend to attack or bite.

1. Friendly or playful body language:

Friendly

☐ Total body is moving side to side while moving forward in a relaxed way.

☐ Face is relaxed while moving.

☐ Mouth is opening and closing, relaxed.

☐ Dog is bouncing off the ground with its body swinging.

☐ Front legs are stretched out forward with rear end in the air so that the dog appears to be bowing with its whole body wiggling.

☐ Dog is moving forward then stopping, while bouncing from side to side.

2. Potentially threatening body language:

☐ Dog's head is turned but it is still looking at you.

☐ Dog is circling you, attempting to attack from behind. *Good time to utilize dog repellent spray.*

☐ Head is carried high or low — high head shows a dominant dog; low head shows a fearful dog.

☐ Dog is looking back and forth quickly, while retreating (shows a nervous or fearful dog).

☐ Could be barking or silent; it does not matter which.

Potentially threatening

☐ Mouth is tensed when closed with lips pulled back tight — could be growling.

☐ Front legs are stretched out forward with rear end in the air so that the dog appears to be bowing, *but its body is stiff, not moving.*

3. Dangerous body language:

☐ A surge of adrenaline will surface, and the dog's body will stiffen. The stiffness will happen whether the dog is moving or still.

☐ Hackles (hair along the neck and spine) will rise.

☐ Teeth could be showing. Dogs with large muzzle skin will seldom show teeth because they are unable to lift the muzzle skin.

☐ Dog maintains direct eye contact that results in tunnel vision. The dog doesn't get distracted by any other movement around it and is unable to hear its owner's commands.

☐ Dog is barking and not moving, trying to warn you to stay away.

☐ The dog's tail could be wagging because it is happy and excited about biting you. A dog with its tail tucked under may bite you out of fear.

Dangerous

☐ The dog makes a fast, direct approach then stops; its next approach may be to bite you. *Good time to utilize dog repellent spray.*

Review of alternatives to deadly force:

☐ Evaluate the dog's body language to determine if a threat exists.

☐ Use the defensive tactics described above.

☐ Use dog repellent spray.

☐ Strike the dog.

☐ Use a fire extinguisher.

☐ Use a taser.

FIRE FIGHTERS, AMBULANCE DRIVERS, PARAMEDICS AND FIRST RESPONDERS

Any dog can be a threat. All dogs will bite when protecting themselves, their property, and/or their owners. Since dogs can't talk, they may bite to tell you "No" or "Stop," — even if it's your own dog.

How can you tell the difference between a dog encounter and an attack? In a dog encounter, the dog will confront you but decide not to attack. In an attack the dog has decided to bite you. It's hard to tell when a dog encounter will turn into an attack. Sometimes you surprise a dog and it will attack right away, or it may first try to warn you off. You can't know what any dog will do in the face of stress, so you have to be prepared for both a harmless encounter and an actual attack when you meet a dog. You don't want to injure or kill a harmless dog, but you don't want to get bitten either. The detailed instructions and checklists that follow will help you know what is best to do in a simple encounter and an outright attack.

How to avoid the five deadly sins of dog encounters:

- Never assume all dogs are friendly. A dog's behavior can change suddenly without any warning. Dogs under stress are unpredictable, and even cute dogs will bite.
- Never run from any dog — running triggers the dog's hunting instinct.
- Never turn your back on any dog. The dog may already be afraid. If you turn away or run, the dog's instinct will tell it to chase you and bite you out of its own fear. Such a dog is a fear-biter.
- Don't depend on the owner to know how his dog will behave under stress.
- Don't stand face to face with a dog during a threat. This will only challenge the dog to a fight.

When arriving at a location check for:

- ☐ "Beware of Dog" signs
- ☐ dog house, chains, bowls
- ☐ dog feces in yard — the smell may strike you before you actually see them
- ☐ worn track around fence — an indication that the dog is out a lot
- ☐ sleeping or unalert dog — shake fence or make any noise to alert or wake up the dog.
- ☐ If the dog is tied up and you have to cross its path, be cautious and ready to protect yourself, because an aggressive dog may get a burst of strength and break its rope or chain.

Vehicles entering the dog owner's yard:

Dogs have learned that a vehicle entering their property signals someone approaching the house. A dog will hear or see the intruder and begin barking, challenging the person and warning him to stay away. The dog often continues barking until the person gets in his vehicle and drives away. When this happens, the dog believes it has done its job by scaring the intruder away. It has won its challenge.

This barking ritual can build an adrenaline high that could make the dog break through a window or door and at worst trigger a bite if the dog gets loose. You will need to be ready to defend yourself against such a dog if this happens. See below for the sections on defensive tactics for dog encounters and attacks.

Why dogs bark at doorbell rings and knocks at the door:

The dog has learned that the doorbell or a knock at the door means someone is on the other side. The dog will bark either because the person is invading its territory or because it is excited about meeting the person. Either way, the dog begins to associate the doorbell or knock with someone arriving. If the dog barks to protect its territory, it will believe it has won once the person leaves, making the dog confident that its bark has scared away the invader. The next time someone knocks or rings the doorbell, the dog will bark more intensely. If the person enters the house, the dog may either continue feeling aggressive about the invader or switch to being friendly because the new person gives it positive attention, touches it and makes friends with it.

If the dog has been barking out of excitement, it learns that when the person comes in, it will be rewarded with a touch and attention. This will make the dog bark more intensely the next time because it gets excited about the idea that the person will enter and give it friendly attention.

If owner is present:

☐ Insist the dog be placed in a secure area. Try saying, "I *need* you to put the dog away." If the owner resists, you could try saying, "I would feel better if you would put your dog away."

☐ Never pet the dog. You are not part of the dog's social order, and it may bite you even if you have petted it before.

☐ Avoid quick movements. The dog could be nervous, and a quick movement will trigger its fear-biting response.

If the dog is guarding its owner while the owner is unresponsive:

The dog views anyone approaching its owner as a threat. If its owner is unresponsive, the dog may become aware of its owner's vulnerability and will become aggressive to keep you away. The dog has no idea that you are trying to assist its owner or save his life. It is only doing what comes instinctively. Some dogs will even lie right on top of their owners when they are guarding them or at least stay firmly by their side. Others will refuse to let anyone enter their yard or house. Your goal is to remove the dog without using deadly force. Here is how you can approach the dog:

☐ First evaluate the dog's body language. The dog may be comforting the owner, or it may be a threat to you. See the last section in this chapter, "How to understand a dog's body language."

☐ While approaching the dog, speak to it in a calm voice and wait for a friendly response in body language, such as a relaxed head and body.

☐ If the dog is friendly, you should still secure it, because the dog could switch to being aggressive at any time.

☐ If the dog is charging and then retreating to its owner, use a barrier such as a chair, backboard or heavy sheet to block the dog from biting you.

☐ Use a ladder or other barrier to push the dog into a room or a secure area.

☐ If the dog refuses to move, throw a sheet over it, wrap the sheet around the dog and pull it into another room or secure area.

☐ Don't use repellent spray; it may affect the unresponsive owner.

☐ Don't use a fire extinguisher; it may create a fog that will prevent you from seeing clearly, and its spray may remove oxygen from the air, injuring you and the unresponsive owner.

When giving something to a person with a dog or taking anything from him:

☐ Have the person come to you; this will make the dog invade your space instead of you invading its personal space. A dog may bite you if you invade its space or may perceive your coming towards it as a threat.

☐ Have the person take the object while you hold the object close to you; the dog could perceive your hand reaching out as a threat.

☐ When leaving, do not turn your back on the dog and walk away. Instead, either walk slowly backwards to a safe distance while always keeping your eye on the dog or allow the owner and dog to leave first.

☐ If the dog becomes aggressive at any time, walk backwards to create space and place the object you are trying to give the person somewhere else. Tell the owner to stop coming towards you.

☐ If a screen door is the only door between you and the dog and the dog is jumping on it, place your foot and hand on the door to make sure the dog doesn't force it open.

Defensive tactics against a dog encounter:

☐ Do not run; you will only cause the dog's biting instinct to surface.

☐ Avoid quick movement. The dog could be nervous, and a quick movement may trigger fear-biting.

☐ Stop and stand sideways, so the dog doesn't think you are challenging it.

☐ Give it some common commands ("stay," "sit," "down"). This makes the dog think maybe you are in charge.

☐ If you know the dog, relax it by using its name.

☐ Be careful about giving negative commands ("no," "get out of here"). They may work, but if a dog perceives them as a threat, you may escalate the dog's aggression and get bitten.

☐ If the dog is coming towards you, move backwards and sideways, keeping and eye on the dog. This gives you space and time to react.

☐ Look at the dog, but don't stare into its eyes. Look at the top of its head or at its eyebrows. Looking away may tell the dog it has won the challenge, and it may bite you.

☐ Once the dog loses interest in you, move slowly backwards until you are out of its sight.

☐ Provide the dog room for an escape by not cutting off escape routes such as a door or gate.

☐ Remain calm by taking deep breaths. This will calm your body; dogs can sense tension and fear. If the dog senses your fear (and it probably will), it will gain confidence about biting you.

Defending yourself against a dog attack

☐ Stop stand sideways, so the dog doesn't think you are challenging it.

☐ Evaluate the dog's body language. See "How to understand a dog's body language" at the end of this chapter.

☐ If the dog is attacking, present a moving target by waving something in front of the dog. Walk backwards, keeping an eye on the dog.

☐ If bitten *don't pull away.* This is very difficult to do, but if you pull away, the bite will be much more serious because the dog will resist having anything pulled from its mouth and will fight harder to hold on, causing more skin-tearing and deeper wounds.

☐ Use defensive options in escalating order: verbal commands, dog repellent spray and striking techniques.

☐ As soon as you can, notify Animal Control or the police.

How to use dog repellent spray:

Whatever brand or type of dog repellent spray you decide to use, read the directions carefully. Check the can regularly to make sure it's still in working order. Do this by shaking the contents vigorously and spraying a small amount. Don't spray too much because repeated testing will use up the spray and leave you with too little when you really need it. If it is cold, make sure the brand you use doesn't freeze. Keep it warm by putting it next to your body.

Dog repellent spray is a nonlethal product that temporarily disorients the dog by surprising it. Dogs don't expect you to reach out and touch them without using your hands. The spray also gives the dog a quick liquid sting and causes temporary eye and nose irritation which distracts it. When it feels the irritation, it will attempt to rub off the substance by pawing at it or rolling on the ground. If you spray the repellent in the dog's mouth, it will immediately begin salivating and be distracted from biting. If the wind is low and the repellent's pressure is at full strength, most sprays can reach up to 12 feet.

In my experience, repellent spray works on dogs that have not decided to bite but may do so at any time, such as dogs that are circling you or barking at you but not moving. Don't think the spray is your main line of defense. Dogs that are attacking or are intent on biting you may see it as a threat or a challenge, and in their desire to overcome this challenge will become more aggressive. Such dogs are full of adrenaline and may not feel the spray's effects. When using dog repellent spray:

☐ Remember that although you have been told to spray the dog's eyes, that is an almost impossible target to hit. Compared to humans' eyes, dogs have much larger tear ducts and a third eyelid. These assist them in recovering faster. I have been more successful spraying the dog in the mouth. This stimulates the dog's licking reflex, thus stopping it from biting. Also, the mouth is a much larger target.

☐ If the dog is biting you or has its face very close to you, try spraying into its nostrils. This will instantly cause maximum irritation, and the dog will back off.

☐ Spray in a figure eight motion, creating a continuous wall of spray. This will give you a greater chance of hitting some part of the dog's face.

☐ Start spraying as soon as you see the dog coming at you, assuming you have the can out and are ready to use it. You must be ready, because a delay will allow the dog to get too close to you or actually begin biting you.

☐ Walk slowly backwards, keeping an eye on the dog. This creates space and gives you time to think about your other options. See below for how to use striking techniques.

☐ Give verbal obedience commands to the dog ("sit," "down" or "stay") as you are walking slowly backwards.

☐ While walking backwards, you are also escaping. Some dogs think they have done their jobs when you have gone away from their territory.

Fighting back an attack using striking techniques:

During an attack or if an attack is imminent, you may decide to use striking techniques. Your objective is to destroy the dog's confidence by striking it with dramatic, instant, painful strikes and to survive the encounter with the least amount of injury to yourself. If you think you can't strike the dog effectively, don't use this option. The dog may view your ineffective strikes as a challenge, which will make it fight even harder, thus increasing your chance of injury.

How to use striking techniques:

☐ Knee or kick the dog in the chest; this will knock the wind out of it.

☐ If possible get the dog's attention by moving something over your head; this will get the dog to focus on the moving target and expose its chest.

☐ Punch, chop or strike the back of the neck where the shoulders meet, or aim for the spine. Use any device that will make an impact.

☐ Use your forearm to punch downward on the dog's spine or drive downward with your body weight going to the ground.

☐ Give an upper cut to the throat.

☐ Slam the dog to the ground or up against a wall.

☐ Keep an eye on the dog at all times.

☐ If the dog retreats, walk backwards to an escape route.

| Kick or knee to the chest | Punch back of the neck where the shoulders meet | Punch downward with forearm to the spine | Uppercut to the throat |

Using a fire extinguisher against a dog attack:

☐ Disables the dog temporarily.

☐ Restricts oxygen intake temporarily.

☐ Is most effective when you spray in two to three second bursts.

☐ Has little to no effect on dogs that are fighting.

☐ *But,* used indoors, it may create fog or remove oxygen from the air and temporarily incapacitate you.

Gaining entry to a house with a dog inside:

☐ Have back-up fire fighter carry a fire extinguisher. If you are alone, wait for backup.

☐ Make sure the dog has an escape route.

☐ If possible and if the backyard is fenced, have the second fire fighter open back door to let the dog outside.

☐ If you can't let the dog out, use the second fire fighter to distract the dog by throwing a blanket over it or pushing it into another room with the backboard.

☐ Keep your eye on the dog at all times.

☐ If available, use a shield or an ambulance backboard to push the dog into another room.

☐ Use lethal force as a last resort only. The dog is doing its job by protecting its owner and property.

Gaining entry into a vehicle with a dog inside during an emergency such as a serious accident:

☐ Evaluate the dog's condition. Is it bleeding, limping, not moving? If the dog is injured, notify Animal Control. In the meantime, use a backboard or shield to block the dog.

☐ If the vehicle's doors are open, allow the dog to escape; then notify Animal Control.

☐ If time and circumstances permit, notify Animal Control to remove the dog.

☐ Use a shield or ambulance backboard to block or push dog out of the car.

☐ If the car doors are locked, break two windows: the first one for opening the door and the second one to give the dog an escape route.

☐ Use a second fire fighter for a distraction to get the victim out of the vehicle.

☐ Use lethal force as a last resort only. The dog is only doing its job by protecting its owner and the car.

Loose dogs and stray dogs (notify Animal Control or the local police):

A loose dog or a stray dog has been allowed to determine its own territory. The dog now believes its roaming area, regardless of the size, belongs to it. This makes the dog unpredictable even if it appears friendly. Anyone invading its territory will make the dog protect it, so stay away from all stray dogs and notify Animal Control or the police.

Dogs trained for protection:

While being trained to protect its owner and her property, the dog has always been allowed to win. Because of this, the dog's confidence has been so strongly built up that it thinks it can overcome anything a human can give out. Be prepared to divert the dog's attention from you to a target object that it can defeat, such as a hat or sack. While it is attacking the object, it will become vulnerable to your repellent spray, striking techniques or stronger measures.

Dogs not trained for protection:

Similar to a dog trained for protection, a dog not specifically trained for protection will still instinctively protect its house or yard as its territory. It believes that it has won all challenges from people invading its space. After all, it scares you and others away when it barks.

Why dogs try to scare off people in uniforms:

If you are wearing a uniform, you need to know why dogs will react to you by barking. A uniformed person enters the dog's yard. It barks; the person leaves. The dog thinks that it has scared the person away. Thus, uniformed people who come and go as part of their jobs have indirectly built the dog's confidence in its ability to challenge them. Now the dog perceives anyone in uniform who invades its territory as a threat. This makes the dog potentially dangerous even if it appears friendly.

The treat myth:

If you carry treats to smooth things over with some dogs, the dogs will see people entering their property as a good thing. The problem arises when new fire fighters or strangers see a dog running toward them looking for a treat, and they get confused about what the dog intends. They may well think the dog is about to attack and will hit it, spray it with repellent or use even stronger force. Your treats have created a painful, even lethal, trap for the dog.

How to understand a dog's body language:

Study the body language of dogs you encounter during work, as well as your own pets. What makes a dog excited? What makes it fearful? What stresses it? What does your behavior contribute to the dog's behavior? Familiarize yourself with other types of dogs with different temperaments and from different breeds. Notice especially how the different kinds of dogs look when they are experiencing various emotions ranging from excitement and joy to fear and aggressiveness. Before long you will begin anticipating a particular dog's behaviors just by the way it looks, and you will be able to do this for the other types of dogs you have studied.

The dog's eyes are very hard to read. Because they are small, you have to get close up to study them. When the dog is afraid or ready to attack, its eyes glare, even if it is excited about biting you. When the dog is happy or excited in a friendly way, its eyes look soft. When the dog is sick or sad, its eyes look weak.

Below are the most common body language signs associated with the behaviors you need to know about. Once these become recognizable, you should begin to expand your knowledge by learning the mixed signals dogs give because of undesirable genetics, incorrect training and poor environment. Also, dogs' body language varies according to whether or not they have a tail or have prick or floppy ears.

Remember that the dog's body language does not lie. It does not use its body language to trap you into getting bitten. Dogs may be master manipulators when they want their way, but, to our advantage, they do not use manipulation when they intend to attack or bite.

1. Friendly or playful body language:

☐ Total body is moving side to side while moving forward in a relaxed way.

☐ Face is relaxed while moving.

☐ Mouth is opening and closing, relaxed.

☐ Dog is bouncing off the ground with its body swinging.

Friendly

☐ Front legs are stretched out forward with rear end in the air so that the dog appears to be bowing with its whole body wiggling.

☐ Dog is moving forward then stopping, while bouncing from side to side.

2. Potentially threatening body language:

☐ Dog's head is turned but it is still looking at you.

☐ Dog is circling you, attempting to attack from behind.

☐ Head is carried high or low — high head shows a dominant dog; low head shows a fearful dog.

☐ Could be barking or silent; it does not matter which.

Potentially threatening

☐ Mouth is tensed when closed with lips pulled back tight — could be growling.

☐ Front legs are stretched out forward with rear end in the air so that the dog appears to be bowing, *but its body is stiff, not moving.*

3. Dangerous body language:

☐ A surge of adrenaline will surface, and the dog's body will stiffen. The stiffness will happen whether the dog is moving or still.

☐ Hackles (hair along the neck and spine) will rise.

☐ Teeth could be showing. Dogs with large muzzle skin will seldom show teeth because they are unable to lift the muzzle skin.

☐ Dog maintains direct eye contact that results in tunnel vision. The dog doesn't get distracted by any other movement around it and is unable to hear its owner's commands.

☐ Dog is barking and not moving, trying to warn you to stay away.

☐ The dog's tail could be wagging because it is happy and excited about biting you. A dog with its tail tucked under may bite you out of fear.

☐ The dog makes a fast, direct approach then stops; its next approach may be to bite you.

Dangerous

LETTER CARRIERS

Any dog can be a threat. All dogs will bite when protecting themselves, their property, and/or their owners. Since dogs can't talk, they may bite to tell you "no" or "stop," — even if it's your own dog.

How can you tell the difference between a dog encounter and an attack? In a dog encounter, the dog will confront you but decide not to attack. In an attack the dog has decided to bite you. It's hard to tell when a dog encounter will turn into an attack. Sometimes you surprise a dog and it will attack right away, or it may first try to warn you off. You can't know what any dog will do in the face of stress, so you have to be prepared for both a harmless encounter and an actual attack when you meet a dog. You don't want to injure or kill a harmless dog, but you don't want to get bitten either. The detailed instructions and checklists that follow will help you know what is best to do in a simple encounter and an outright attack.

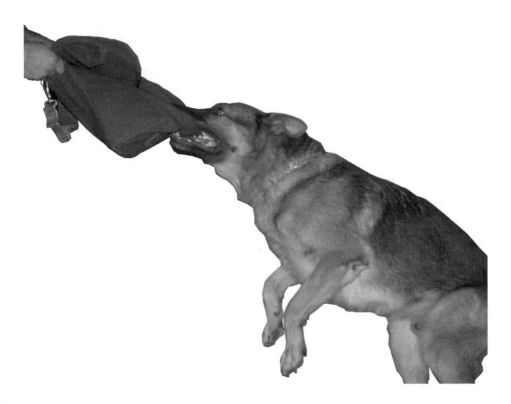

How to avoid the five deadly sins of dog encounters:

- Never assume all dogs are friendly. A dog's behavior can change suddenly without warning. Dogs under stress are unpredictable, and even cute dogs will bite.

- Never run from any dog — running triggers the dog's hunting instinct, making the dog chase you.

- Never turn your back on any dog. The dog may already be afraid. If you turn away or run, the dog's instinct will tell it to chase you and bite you out of its own fear. Such a dog is a fear-biter.

- Don't depend on the owner to know how his dog will behave under stress.

- Don't stand face to face with a dog during a threat. This will only challenge the dog to a fight.

Remember that 90 percent of all dog bites to letter carriers are below the waist, mostly on the legs.[7] This occurs because letter carriers turn away from the dog, or owners are unable to control their dogs after the carrier has turned around to leave. Then, the owner opens the door, and the dog charges out the door and attacks the departing carrier from the back. Taken by surprise, the carrier can't defend himself and gets bitten. Because his legs are at the dog's eye level and are moving, the dog usually targets them.

When arriving at a location check for:

- ☐ "Beware of Dog" signs
- ☐ dog house, chains, bowls
- ☐ dog feces in yard — the smell may strike you before you actually see them
- ☐ worn track around fence — an indication that the dog is out a lot
- ☐ sleeping or unalert dog — shake fence or make any noise to alert or wake up the dog.
- ☐ If the dog is tied up and you have to cross its path, don't do so. An aggressive dog may get a burst of strength and break its rope or chain.
- ☐ If the dog is in a yard where an underground electric fence is confining it, don't consider that type of fence a valid means of containment. The dog may get a rush of adrenaline and cross the fence line. The dog's state of aggression will numb its body from the shock and it may bite you.
- ☐ *Use your discretion. If your safety is at risk, don't deliver the mail. Then explain to your supervisor why you didn't deliver it.*

Vehicles entering the dog owner's yard:

Dogs have learned that a vehicle entering their property signals someone approaching the house. A dog will hear or see the intruder and begin barking, challenging the person and warning him to stay away. The dog often continues barking until the person gets in his

---

[7] United States Post Office, Publicity Kit for "National Dog Bite Prevention Week, May 18-24, 2003." Website: http://www.usps.com/cpim/ftp/bulletin/2003/html/pb22100/kitl.htm.

vehicle and drives away. When this happens, the dog believes it has done its job by scaring the intruder away. It has won its challenge.

This barking ritual can build an adrenaline high that could make the dog break through a window or door and at worst trigger a bite if the dog gets loose. You will need to be ready to defend yourself against such a dog if this happens. See below for the sections on defensive tactics for dog encounters and attacks.

If a dog continues to bark wildly whenever you drive up, notify the owner of the danger that could result should the dog get loose. If the owner fails to take reasonable measures, such as securing the dog away from windows and doors and making sure the dog is not loose when you arrive, refuse to come to the house.

Why dogs bark at doorbell rings and knocks at the door:

The dog has learned that the doorbell or a knock at the door means someone is on the other side. The dog will bark either because the person is invading its territory or because it is excited about meeting the person. Either way, the dog begins to associate the doorbell or knock with someone arriving. If the dog barks to protect its territory, it will believe it has won once the person leaves, making the dog confident that its bark has scared away the invader. The next time someone knocks or rings the doorbell, the dog will bark more intensely. If the person enters the house, the dog may either continue feeling aggressive about the invader or switch to being friendly because the new person gives it positive attention, touches it and makes friends with it.

If the dog has been barking out of excitement, it learns that when the person comes in, it will be rewarded with a touch and attention. This will make the dog bark more intensely the next time because it gets excited about the idea that the person will enter and give it friendly attention.

If owner is present:

- ☐ Insist the dog be placed in a secure area. Try saying, "I *need* you to put the dog away." If the owner resists, you could try saying, "I would feel better if you would put your dog away."

- ☐ Never pet the dog. You are not part of the dog's social order, and it may bite you even if you have petted it before.

- ☐ Avoid quick movements. The dog could be nervous, and a quick movement will trigger its fear-biting response.

- ☐ If the owner answers the door with the dog or the dog shows up during the meeting and becomes aggressive, prevent the dog from escaping and biting by grasping the door and closing it. If time permits tell the owner: "I need to close the door," or "I need you to close the door, because your dog may bite."

- ☐ If the dog becomes aggressive, don't grasp the owner in an attempt to use her as a shield. The dog may view your actions as an attack on the owner and may bite you to protect her.

When giving something to a person with a dog or taking anything from him:

- ☐ Have the person come to you; this will make the dog invade your space instead of you invading its personal space. A dog may bite you if you invade its space or may perceive your coming towards it as a threat.

- ☐ Have the person take the object while you hold the object close to you; the dog could perceive your hand reaching out as a threat.

- ☐ When leaving, do not turn your back on the dog and walk away. Instead, either walk slowly backwards to a safe distance while always keeping your eye on the dog or allow the owner and dog to leave first.

- ☐ If the dog becomes aggressive at any time, walk backwards to create space and place the object you are trying to give the person somewhere else. Tell the owner to stop coming towards you.

- ☐ If a screen door is the only door between you and the dog and the dog is jumping on it, place your foot and hand on the door to make sure the dog doesn't force it open. If the door is broken shout for the owner and/or spray repellent at the dog through the screen. See below for a discussion of how to use dog repellent spray.

- ☐ Don't give mail to a child or take it from her when a dog is present. Dogs know children are vulnerable and may see them as property which needs protecting. A child can bond so closely to her dog that the dog will instinctively protect her as if the child were its own.

Defensive tactics against a dog encounter:

- ☐ Do not run; you will only cause the dog's biting instinct to surface.
- ☐ If a dog is following you; stop and evaluate. The dog may just want to smell you.
- ☐ Stop and stand sideways, so the dog doesn't think you are challenging it.
- ☐ Avoid quick movement. The dog could be nervous and a quick movement may trigger fear-biting.
- ☐ If the dog is coming towards you, move backwards and sideways, keeping an eye on the dog. This gives you space and time to react.

☐ Carry a high-pitched sound device. See below for how to use the device.

☐ Give it some common commands ("stay," "sit," "down"). This makes the dog think maybe you are in charge.

☐ Be careful about giving negative commands ("no," "get out of here"). They may work, but if a dog perceives them as a threat, you may escalate the dog's aggression and get bitten.

☐ Look at the dog, but don't stare into its eyes. Look at the top of its head or at its eyebrows. Looking away may tell the dog it has won the challenge, and it may bite you.

☐ If you know the dog, relax it by using its name.

☐ Once the dog loses interest in you, move slowly backwards until you are out of its sight.

☐ Provide the dog room for an escape by not cutting off escape routes such as a door or gate.

☐ Remain calm by taking deep breaths. This will calm your body; dogs can sense tension and fear. If the dog senses your fear (and it probably will), it will gain confidence about biting you.

☐ If cornered, remain still and wait until the dog loses interest. This usually takes only a few minutes, so be patient. Then move slowly away.

Defending yourself against a dog attack: stop, drop and curl:

If the attack is imminent, fall on the ground and curl up in a ball, protecting your vital organs, face and ears. Do not scream or yell. This will only make the dog more confident. Its survival instinct will surface, and it will attack with renewed force. Once you are on the ground and silent, you are no longer a threat.

If an attack isn't imminent:

☐ Stop and stand sideways so the dog doesn't think you're challenging it.

☐ Evaluate the dog's body language. See "How to understand a dog's body language" at the end of this chapter.

☐ If the dog is attacking, present a moving target by waving something like your satchel in front of the dog. Walk slowly backwards, keeping an eye on the dog.

Don't run or turn your back.

☐ If dog bites satchel or any other moving object, use dog repellent spray, striking techniques or stronger measures.

☐ If bitten *don't pull away.* This is very difficult to do, but if you pull away, the bite will be much more serious because the dog will resist having anything pulled from its mouth and will fight harder to hold on, causing more skin-tearing and deeper wounds.

☐ Use defensive options in escalating order: verbal commands, dog repellent spray, striking techniques or stronger measures.

☐ As soon as you can, notify Animal Control or the police.

How to use dog repellent spray:

Whatever brand or type of dog repellent spray you decide to use, read the directions carefully. Check the can regularly to make sure it's still in working order. Do this by shaking the contents vigorously and spraying a small amount. Don't spray too much because repeated testing will use up the spray and leave you with too little when you really need it. If it is cold, make sure the brand you use doesn't freeze. Keep it warm by putting it next to your body.

Dog repellent spray is a nonlethal product that temporarily disorients the dog by surprising it. Dogs don't expect you to reach out and touch them without using your hands. The spray also gives the dog a quick liquid sting and causes temporary eye and nose irritation which distracts it. When it feels the irritation, it will attempt to rub off the substance by pawing at it or rolling on the ground. If you spray the repellent in the dog's mouth, it will immediately begin salivating and be distracted from biting. If the wind is low and the repellent's pressure is at full strength, most sprays can reach up to 12 feet.

In my experience, repellent spray works on dogs that have not decided to bite but may do so at any time, such as dogs that are circling you or barking at you but not moving. Don't think the spray is your main line of defense. Dogs that are attacking or are intent on biting you may see it as a threat or a challenge, and in their desire to overcome this challenge will become more aggressive. Such dogs are full of adrenaline and may not feel the spray's effects. When using dog repellent spray:

☐ Remember that although you have been told to spray the dog's eyes, that is an almost impossible target to hit. Compared to humans' eyes, dogs have much larger tear ducts and a third eyelid. These assist them in recovering faster. I have been more successful spraying the dog in the mouth. This stimulates the dog's licking reflex, thus stopping it from biting. Also, the mouth is a much larger target.

☐ If the dog is biting you or has its face very close to you, try spraying into its nostrils. This will instantly cause maximum irritation, and the dog will back off.

☐ Spray in a figure eight motion, creating a continuous wall of spray. This will give you a greater chance of hitting some part of the dog's face.

☐ Start spraying as soon as you see the dog coming at you, assuming you have the can out and are ready to use it. You must be ready, because a delay will allow the dog to get too close to you or actually begin biting you.

☐ Walk slowly backwards keeping an eye on the dog. This creates space and gives you time to think about your other options. See below for how to use striking techniques.

☐ Give verbal obedience commands to the dog ("sit," "down" or "stay") as you are walking backwards.

☐ While walking backwards, you are also escaping. Some dogs think they have done their jobs when you have gone away from their territory.

High-pitched sound devices:

These emit a high-pitched tone that humans can't hear but dogs can. The device should be used as soon as the dog encounter becomes threatening. These devices cause discomfort to the dog's hearing but have no negative aftereffects. They are about the size of a garage-door opener and fit in the palm of your hand or clip onto your waistband or belt. When you push the activating button, the dog first becomes surprised because it can't tell where the high-pitched sound is coming from. Then it quickly realizes that as it gets closer to you, the sound gets more intense. Being surprised and disturbed by the sound, the dog may not come any closer to you. This device doesn't work on all dogs, but it is an effective protection against dogs that have not yet decided to bite you but could do so at any moment.

Fighting back an attack using striking techniques:

During an attack or if an attack is imminent, you may decide to use striking techniques. Your objective is to destroy the dog's confidence by striking it with dramatic, instant, painful strikes and to survive the encounter with the least amount of injury to yourself. If you think you can't strike the dog effectively, don't use this option. The dog may view your ineffective strikes as a challenge, which will make it fight even harder, thus increasing your chance of injury.

| *Kick or knee to the chest* | *Punch back of the neck where the shoulders meet* | *Punch downward with forearm to the spine* | *Uppercut to the throat* |

How to use striking techniques:

- ☐ Knee or kick the dog in the chest; this will knock the wind out of it.
- ☐ If possible get the dog's attention by moving something over your head; this will get the dog to focus on the moving target and expose its chest.
- ☐ Punch, chop or strike the back of the neck where the shoulders meet, or aim for the spine. Use any device that will make an impact.
- ☐ Use your forearm to punch downward on the dog's spine or drive downward with your body weight going to the ground.
- ☐ Give an upper cut to the throat.
- ☐ Slam the dog to the ground or up against a wall.
- ☐ Keep an eye on the dog at all times.
- ☐ If the dog retreats, walk backwards to an escape route.

Loose dogs and stray dogs (notify Animal Control or the local police):

A loose dog or a stray dog has been allowed to determine its own territory. The dog now believes its roaming area, regardless of the size, belongs to it. This makes the dog unpredictable even if it appears friendly. Anyone invading its territory will make the dog protect it, so stay away from all stray dogs and notify Animal Control or the police.

Dogs trained for protection:

While being trained to protect its owner and her property, the dog has always been allowed to win. Because of this, the dog's confidence has been so strongly built up that it thinks it can overcome anything a human can give out. Be prepared to divert the dog's attention from you to a target object that it can defeat, such as a hat or sack. While it is attacking the object, it will become vulnerable to your repellent spray, striking techniques or stronger measures.

Dogs not trained for protection:

Similar to a dog trained for protection, a dog not specifically trained for protection will still instinctively protect its house or yard as its territory. It believes that it has won all challenges from people invading its space. After all, it scares you and others away when it barks.

Why dogs try to scare off people in uniforms:

If you are wearing a uniform, you need to know why dogs react to you by barking. A uniformed person enters the dog's yard. It barks; the person leaves. The dog thinks that it has scared him away. Thus, uniformed people who come and go as part of their jobs have indirectly built the dog's confidence in its ability to challenge them. Now the dog perceives anyone wearing a uniform who invades its territory as a threat. This makes the dog potentially dangerous even if it appears friendly.

The treat myth:

If you carry treats to smooth things over with some dogs, the dogs will see people entering their property as a good thing. The problem arises when new mail carriers or strangers get confused by the approaching dog. The dog is looking for its treat, but the stranger may well think the dog is about to attack and will hit it, spray it with repellent or use even stronger force. Your treats have created a painful, even lethal, trap for the dog.

How to understand a dog's body language:

Study the body language of the dogs you encounter during work, as well as your own pets. What makes a dog excited? What makes it fearful? What stresses it? What does your behavior contribute to the dog's behavior? Familiarize yourself with other types of dogs with different temperaments and from different breeds. Notice especially how the different kinds of dogs look when they are experiencing various emotions ranging from excitement and joy to fear and aggressiveness. Before long you will begin anticipating a particular dog's behaviors just by the way it looks, and you will be able to do this for the other types of dogs you have studied.

The dog's eyes are very hard to read. Because they are small, you have to get close up to study them. When the dog is afraid or ready to attack, its eyes glare, even if it is excited about biting you. When the dog is happy or excited in a friendly way, its eyes look soft. When the dog is sick or sad, its eyes look weak.

Below are the most common body language signs associated with the behaviors you need to know about. Once these become recognizable, you should begin to expand your knowledge by learning the mixed signals dogs give because of undesirable genetics, incorrect training and poor environment. Also, dogs' body language varies according to whether or not they have a tail or have prick or floppy ears.

Remember that the dog's body language does not lie. It does not use its body language to trap you into getting bitten. Dogs may be master manipulators when they want their way, but, to our advantage, they do not use manipulation when they intend to attack or bite.

1. Friendly or playful body language:

- [ ] Total body is moving side to side while moving forward in a relaxed way.
- [ ] Face is relaxed while dog is moving.
- [ ] Mouth is opening and closing, relaxed.
- [ ] Dog is bouncing off the ground with body swinging.

Friendly

- [ ] Front legs are stretched out forward with rear end in the air so that the dog appears to be bowing with its whole body wiggling.
- [ ] Dog is moving forward then stopping, while bouncing from side to side.

2. Potentially threatening body language:

☐ Dog's head is turned but the dog is still looking at you.

☐ Dog is circling you, attempting to attack from behind. *Good time to utilize dog repellent spray or high-pitched sound devices.*

☐ Head is carried high or low — high head shows a dominant dog; low head shows a fearful dog.

Potentially threatening

☐ Could be barking or silent; it does not matter which.

☐ Mouth is tensed when closed with lips curled tight — could be growling.

☐ Front legs are stretched out forward with rear end in the air so that the dog appears to be bowing, *but its body is stiff, not moving.*

3. Dangerous body language:

☐ A surge of adrenaline will surface, and the dog's body will stiffen. The stiffness will happen whether the dog is moving or still.

☐ Hackles (hair along the neck and spine) will rise.

☐ Teeth could be showing. Dogs with large muzzle skin will seldom show teeth because they are unable to lift the muzzle skin.

☐ Dog maintains direct eye contact that results in tunnel vision. The dog doesn't get distracted by any other movement around it and is unable to hear its owner's commands.

Dangerous

☐ Dog is barking and not moving, trying to warn you to stay away.

☐ The dog's tail could be wagging because it is happy and excited about biting you. A dog with its tail tucked under may bite you out of fear.

☐ The dog makes a fast, direct approach then stops; its next approach may be to bite you. *Good time to utilize dog repellent spray or high-pitched sound devices.*

Keep in mind:

If the attack is imminent and you are knocked down to the ground, curl up in a protective ball. It is not instinctive for a single, domesticated dog, or dogs without a strong killing instinct, to attack its prey when its prey is motionless. This is the same concept that you may have learned about bear attacks. Usually, neither a bear nor a dog will attack a motionless person or prey. This does not hold true for dogs with a strong killing instinct, however. For a description of how they behave, see the chapter on "Dogs That Are Dangerous or Fighters, Because of Breeding or Learned Behavior."

UTILITY WORKERS

Any dog can be a threat. All dogs will bite when protecting themselves, their property, and/or their owners. Since dogs can't talk, they may bite to tell you "no" or "stop," — even if it's your own dog.

How can you tell the difference between a dog encounter and an attack? In a dog encounter, the dog will confront you but decide not to attack. In an attack the dog has decided to bite you. It's hard to tell when a dog encounter will turn into an attack. Sometimes you surprise a dog and it will attack right away, or it may first try to warn you off. You can't know what any dog will do in the face of stress, so you have to be prepared for both a harmless encounter and an actual attack when you meet a dog. You don't want to injure or kill a harmless dog, but you don't want to get bitten either. The detailed instructions and checklists that follow will help you know what is best to do in a simple encounter and an outright attack.

How to avoid the five deadly sins of dog encounters:

- Never assume all dogs are friendly. A dog's behavior can change suddenly without warning. Dogs under stress are unpredictable, and even cute dogs will bite.

- Never run from any dog — running triggers the dog's hunting instinct.

- Never turn your back on any dog. The dog may already be afraid. If you turn away or run, the dog's instinct will tell it to chase you and bite you out of its own fear. Such a dog is a fear-biter.

- Don't depend on the owner to know how his dog will behave under stress.

- Don't stand face to face with a dog during a threat. This will only challenge the dog to a fight.

When arriving at a location check for:

- ☐ "Beware of Dog" signs
- ☐ dog house, chains, bowls
- ☐ dog feces in yard — the smell may strike you before you actually see them
- ☐ worn track around fence — an indication that the dog is out a lot
- ☐ sleeping or unalert dog — shake fence or make any noise to alert or wake up the dog.
- ☐ If the dog is tied up and you have to cross its path, don't do so. An aggressive dog may get a burst of strength and break its rope or chain.
- ☐ If the dog is in a yard where an underground electric fence is confining it don't consider that type of fence a valid means of containment. The dog may get a rush of adrenaline and cross the fence line. The dog's state of aggression will numb its body from the shock and it may bite you.
- ☐ *Use your discretion. If your safety is at risk refuse and reschedule.*

Vehicles entering the dog owner's yard:

Dogs have learned that a vehicle entering their property signals someone approaching the house. A dog will hear or see the intruder and begin barking, challenging the person and warning him to stay away. The dog often continues barking until the person gets in his vehicle and drives away. When this happens, the dog believes it has done its job by scaring the intruder away. It has won its challenge.

This barking ritual can build an adrenaline high that could make the dog break through a window or door and at worst trigger a bite if the dog gets loose. You will need to be ready to defend yourself against such a dog if this happens. See below for the sections on defensive tactics for dog encounters and attacks.

If a dog continues to bark wildly whenever you drive up, notify the owner of the danger that could result should the dog get loose. If the owner fails to take reasonable measures, such as securing the dog away from windows and doors and making sure the dog is not loose when you arrive, refuse to come to the house.

Why dogs bark at doorbell rings and knocks at the door:

The dog has learned that the doorbell or a knock at the door means someone is on the other side. The dog will bark either because the person is invading its territory or because it is excited about meeting the person. Either way, the dog begins to associate the doorbell or knock with someone arriving. If the dog barks to protect its territory, it will believe it has won once the person leaves, making the dog confident that its bark has scared away the invader. The next time someone knocks or rings the doorbell, the dog will bark more intensely. If the person enters the house, the dog may either continue feeling aggressive about the invader or switch to being friendly because the new person gives it positive attention, touches it and makes friends with it.

If the dog has been barking out of excitement, it learns that when the person comes in, it will be rewarded with a touch and attention. This will make the dog bark more intensely the next time because it gets excited about the idea that the person will enter and give it friendly attention.

If owner is present:

- ☐ Insist the dog be placed in a secure area. Try saying, "I *need* you to put the dog away." If the owner resists, you could try saying, "I would feel better if you would put your dog away."

- ☐ Never pet the dog. You are not part of the dog's social order, and it may bite you even if you have petted it before.

- ☐ Avoid quick movements. The dog could be nervous, and a quick movement will trigger its fear-biting response.

- ☐ If the owner answers the door with the dog or the dog shows up during the meeting and becomes aggressive, prevent the dog from escaping and biting by grasping the door and closing it. If time permits tell the owner: "I need to close the door," or "I need you to close the door, because your dog may bite".

- ☐ If the dog becomes aggressive, don't grasp the owner in an attempt to use her as a shield. The dog may view your actions as an attack on the owner and may bite you to protect her.

When giving something to a person with a dog or taking anything from him:

- ☐ Have the person come to you; this will make the dog invade your space instead of you invading its personal space. A dog may bite you if you invade its space or may perceive your coming towards it as a threat.

- ☐ Have the person take the object while you hold the object close to you; the dog could perceive your hand reaching out as a threat.

- ☐ When leaving, do not turn your back on the dog and walk away. Instead, either walk slowly backwards to a safe distance while always keeping your eye on the dog or allow the owner and dog to leave first.

- ☐ If the dog becomes aggressive at any time, walk backwards to create space and place the object you are trying to give the person somewhere else. Tell the owner to stop coming towards you.

☐ If a screened door is the only door between you and the dog and the dog is jumping on it, place your foot and hand on the door to make sure the dog doesn't force it open. If the door is broken shout for the owner and/or spray repellent at the dog through screen. See below for a discussion of how to use dog repellent spray.

Defensive tactics against a dog encounter:

☐ Do not run; you will only cause the dog's biting instinct to surface.

☐ If a dog is following you; stop and evaluate. The dog may just want to smell you.

☐ Stop and stand sideways, so the dog doesn't think you are challenging it.

☐ Avoid quick movement. The dog could be nervous and a quick movement may trigger fear-biting.

☐ If the dog is coming towards you, move backwards and sideways, keeping an eye on the dog. This gives you space and time to react.

☐ Carry a high-pitched sound device. See below for how to use the device.

☐ Give it some common commands ("stay," "sit," "down"). This makes the dog think maybe you are in charge.

☐ Be careful about giving negative commands ("no," "get out of here"). They may work, but if a dog perceives them as a threat, you may escalate the dog's aggression and get bitten.

☐ Look at the dog, but don't stare into its eyes. Look at the top of its head or at its eyebrows. Looking away may tell the dog it has won the challenge, and it may bite you.

☐ If you know the dog, relax it by using its name.

☐ Once the dog loses interest in you, move slowly backwards until you are out of its sight.

☐ Provide the dog room for an escape by not cutting off escape routes such as a door or gate.

☐ Remain calm by taking deep breaths. This will calm your body; dogs can sense tension and fear. If the dog senses your fear (and it probably will), it will gain confidence about biting you.

☐ If cornered, remain still and wait until the dog loses interest. This usually takes only a few minutes, so be patient. Then move slowly away.

If a dog is present in an area where you have to work:

☐ Have your supervisor call the home and ask the owner to put the dog in a secure area.

☐ If no one is home, spend some time reading the dog's body language. See the end of this chapter for a discussion of "How to read a dog's body language."

☐ If you believe the dog is dangerous, refuse to work until the owner makes arrangements to secure the dog.

Defending yourself against a dog attack: stop, drop and curl:

If the attack is imminent, fall on the ground and curl up in a ball, protecting your vital organs, face and ears. Do not scream or yell. This will only make the dog more confident. Its survival instinct will surface, and it will attack with renewed force. Once you are on the ground and silent, you are no longer a threat. If an attack isn't imminent:

Don't run or turn your back.

☐ Stop stand sideways, so the dog doesn't think you are challenging it.

☐ Evaluate the dog's body language.

☐ If the dog is attacking, present a moving target by waving something in front of the dog. Walk slowly backwards, keeping an eye on the dog.

☐ If bitten *don't pull away*. This is very difficult to do, but if you pull away, the bite will be much more serious because the dog will resist having anything pulled from its mouth and will fight harder to hold on, causing more skin-tearing and deeper wounds.

☐ Use defensive options in escalating order: verbal commands, dog repellent spray, striking techniques or stronger measures.

☐ As soon as you can, notify Animal Control or the police.

How to use dog repellent spray:

Whatever brand or type of dog repellent spray you decide to use, read the directions carefully. Check the can regularly to make sure it's still in working order. Do this by shaking the contents vigorously and spraying a small amount. Don't spray too much because repeated testing will use up the spray and leave you with too little when you really need it. If it is cold, make sure the brand you use doesn't freeze. Keep it warm by putting it next to your body.

Dog repellent spray is a nonlethal product that temporarily disorients the dog by surprising it. Dogs don't expect you to reach out and touch them without using your hands. The spray also gives the dog a quick liquid sting and causes temporary eye and nose irritation which distracts it. When it feels the irritation, it will attempt to rub off the substance by pawing at it or rolling on the ground. If you spray the repellent in the dog's mouth, it will immediately begin salivating and be distracted from biting. If the wind is low and the repellent's pressure is at full strength, most sprays can reach up to 12 feet.

In my experience, repellent spray works on dogs that have not decided to bite but may do so at any time, such as dogs that are circling you or barking at you but not moving. Don't think the spray is your main line of defense. Dogs that are attacking or are intent on biting you may see it as a threat or a challenge, and in their desire to overcome this challenge will become more aggressive. Such dogs are full of adrenaline and may not feel the spray's effects. When using dog repellent spray:

- ☐ Remember that although you have been told to spray the dog's eyes, that is an almost impossible target to hit. Compared to humans' eyes, dogs have much larger tear ducts and a third eyelid. These assist them in recovering faster. I have been more successful spraying the dog in the mouth. This stimulates the dog's licking reflex, thus stopping it from biting. Also, the mouth is a much larger target.

- ☐ If the dog is biting you or has its face very close to you, try spraying into its nostrils. This will instantly cause maximum irritation, and the dog will back off.

- ☐ Spray in a figure eight motion, creating a continuous wall of spray. This will give you a greater chance of hitting some part of the dog's face.

- ☐ Start spraying as soon as you see the dog coming at you, assuming you have the can out and are ready to use it. You must be ready, because a delay will allow the dog to get too close to you or actually begin biting you.

- ☐ Walk slowly backwards keeping an eye on the dog. This creates space and gives you time to think about your other options. See below for how to use striking techniques.

- ☐ Give verbal obedience commands to the dog ("sit," "down" or "stay") as you are walking backwards.

- ☐ While walking backwards, you are also escaping. Some dogs think they have done their jobs when you have gone away from their territory.

High-pitched sound devices:

These emit a high-pitched tone that humans can't hear but dogs can. The device should be used as soon as the dog encounter becomes threatening. These devices cause discomfort to the dog's hearing but have no negative aftereffects. They are about the size of a garage-door opener and fit in the palm of your hand or clip onto your waistband or belt. When you push the activating button, the dog first becomes surprised because it can't tell where the high-pitched sound is coming from. Then it quickly realizes that as it gets closer to you, the sound gets more intense. Being surprised and disturbed by the sound, the dog may not come any closer to you. This device doesn't work on all dogs, but it is an effective protection against dogs that have not yet decided to bite you but could do so at any moment.

Fighting back an attack using striking techniques:

During an attack or if an attack is imminent, you may decide to use striking techniques. Your objective is to destroy the dog's confidence by striking it with dramatic, instant, painful strikes and to survive the encounter with the least amount of injury to yourself. If you think you can't strike the dog effectively, don't use this option. The dog may view your ineffective strikes as a challenge, which will make it fight even harder, thus increasing your chance of injury.

| **Kick or knee to the chest** | **Punch back of the neck where the shoulders meet** | **Punch downward with forearm to the spine** | **Uppercut to the throat** |

How to use striking techniques:

☐ Knee or kick the dog in the chest; this will knock the wind out of it.

☐ If possible get the dog's attention by moving something over your head; this will get the dog to focus on the moving target and expose its chest.

☐ Punch, chop or strike the back of the neck where the shoulders meet, or aim for the spine. Use any device that will make an impact.

☐ Use your forearm to punch downward on the dog's spine or drive downward with your body weight going to the ground.

☐ Give an upper cut to the throat.

☐ Slam the dog to the ground or up against a wall.

☐ Keep an eye on the dog at all times.

☐ If the dog retreats, walk slowly backwards to an escape route.

Loose dogs and stray dogs (notify Animal Control or the local police):

A loose dog or a stray dog has been allowed to determine its own territory. The dog now believes its roaming area, regardless of the size, belongs to it. This makes the dog unpredictable even if it appears friendly. Anyone invading its territory will make the dog protect it, so stay away from all stray dogs and notify Animal Control or the police.

Dogs trained for protection:

While being trained to protect its owner and her property, the dog has always been allowed to win. Because of this, the dog's confidence has been so strongly built up that it thinks it can overcome anything a human can give out. Be prepared to divert the dog's attention from you to a target object that it can defeat, such as a hat or sack. While it is attacking the object, it will become vulnerable to your repellent spray, striking techniques or stronger measures.

Dogs not trained for protection:

Similar to a dog trained for protection, a dog not specifically trained for protection will still instinctively protect its house or yard as its territory. It believes that it has won all challenges from people invading its space. After all, it scares you and others away when it barks.

Why dogs try to scare off people in uniforms:

If you are wearing a uniform, you need to know why dogs will react to you by barking. A uniformed person enters the dog's yard. It barks; the person leaves. The dog thinks that it has scared them away. Thus, uniformed people who come and go as part of their jobs have indirectly built the dog's confidence in its ability to challenge them. Now the dog perceives anyone wearing a uniform who invades its territory as a threat. This makes the dog potentially dangerous even if it appears friendly.

The treat myth:

If you carry treats to smooth things over with some dogs, the dogs will see people entering their property as a good thing. The problem arises when new utility workers see a dog running toward them looking for a treat, and they get confused about what the dog intends. The dog is looking for its treat, but the new utility worker may well think it is about to attack and will hit it, spray it with dog repellent or use even stronger force. Your treats have created a painful, even lethal, trap for the dog.

How to understand a dog's body language:

Study the body language of dogs you encounter during work, as well as your own pets. What makes a dog excited? What makes it fearful? What stresses it? What does your behavior contribute to the dog's behavior? Familiarize yourself with other types of dogs with different temperaments and from different breeds. Notice especially how the different kinds of dogs look when they are experiencing various emotions ranging from excitement and joy to fear and aggressiveness. Before long you will begin anticipating a particular dog's behaviors just by the way it looks, and you will be able to do this for the other types of dogs you have studied.

The dog's eyes are very hard to read. Because they are small, you have to get close up to study them. When the dog is afraid or ready to attack, its eyes glare, even if it is excited about biting you. When the dog is happy or excited in a friendly way, its eyes look soft. When the dog is sick or sad, its eyes look weak.

Below are the most common body language signs associated with the behaviors you need to know about. Once these become recognizable, you should begin to expand your knowledge by learning the mixed signals dogs give because of undesirable genetics, incorrect training and poor environment. Also, dogs' body language varies according to whether or not they have a tail or have prick or floppy ears.

Remember that the dog's body language does not lie. It does not use its body language to trap you into getting bitten. Dogs may be master manipulators when they want their way, but, to our advantage, they do not use manipulation when they intend to attack or bite.

1. Friendly or playful body language:

☐ Total body is moving side to side while moving forward in a relaxed way.

☐ Face is relaxed while dog is moving.

☐ Mouth is opening and closing, relaxed.

☐ Dog is bouncing off the ground with body swinging.

☐ Front legs are stretched out forward with rear end in the air so that the dog appears to be bowing with its whole body wiggling.

Friendly

☐ Dog is moving forward then stopping, while bouncing from side to side.

2. Potentially threatening body language:

☐ Dog's head is turned but the dog is still looking at you.

☐ Dog is circling you, attempting to attack from behind. *Good time to utilize dog repellent spray or high-pitched sound devices.*

Potentially threatening

☐ Head is carried high or low — high head shows a dominant dog; low head shows a fearful dog.

☐ Could be barking or silent; it does not matter which.

☐ Mouth is tensed when closed with lips curled tight — could be growling.

☐ Front legs are stretched out forward with rear end in the air so that the dog appears to be bowing, *but its body is stiff, not moving*.

3. Dangerous body language:

☐ A surge of adrenaline will surface, and the dog's body will stiffen. The stiffness will happen whether the dog is moving or still.

☐ Hackles (hair along the neck and spine) will rise.

☐ Teeth could be showing. Dogs with large muzzle skin will seldom show teeth because they are unable to lift the muzzle skin.

Dangerous

- ☐ Dog maintains direct eye contact that results in tunnel vision. The dog doesn't get distracted by any other movement around it and is unable to hear its owner's commands.
- ☐ Dog is barking and not moving, trying to warn you to stay away.
- ☐ The dog's tail could be wagging because it is happy and excited about biting you. A dog with its tail tucked under may bite you out of fear.
- ☐ The dog makes a fast, direct approach then stops; its next approach may be to bite you. *Good time to utilize dog repellent spray or high-pitched sound devices.*

Keep in mind:

If the attack is imminent and you are knocked down to the ground, curl up in a protective ball. It is not instinctive for a single, domesticated dog, or dogs without a strong killing instinct, to attack its prey when its prey is motionless. This is the same concept that you may have learned about bear attacks. Usually, neither a bear nor a dog will attack a motionless person or prey. This does not hold true for dogs with a strong killing instinct, however. For a description of how they behave, see the chapter on "Dogs That Are Dangerous or Fighters, Because of Breeding or Learned Behavior."

PREPARING YOURSELF
FOR DOG ENCOUNTERS FOR:

DELIVERY PERSONNEL

Any dog can be a threat. All dogs will bite when protecting themselves, their property, and/or their owners. Since dogs can't talk, they may bite to tell you "No" or "Stop" — even if it's your own dog.

How can you tell the difference between a dog encounter and an attack? In a dog encounter, the dog will confront you but decide not to attack. In an attack the dog has decided to bite you. It's hard to tell when a dog encounter will turn into an attack. Sometimes you surprise a dog and it will attack right away, or it may first try to warn you off. You can't

know what any dog will do in the face of stress, so you have to be prepared for both a harmless encounter and an actual attack when you meet a dog. You don't want to injure or kill a harmless dog, but you don't want to get bitten either. The detailed instructions and checklists that follow will help you know what is best to do in a simple encounter and an outright attack.

How to avoid the five deadly sins of dog encounters:

- Never assume all dogs are friendly. A dog's behavior can change suddenly without warning. Dogs under stress are unpredictable, and even cute dogs will bite.

- Never run from any dog — running triggers the dog's hunting instinct.

- Never turn your back on any dog. The dog may already be afraid. If you turn away or run, the dog's instinct will tell it to chase you and bite you out of its own fear. Such a dog is a fear-biter.

- Don't depend on the owner to know how his dog will behave under stress.

- Don't stand face to face with a dog during a threat. This will only challenge the dog to a fight.

When arriving at a location check for:

- ☐ "Beware of Dog" signs

- ☐ dog house, chains, bowls

- ☐ dog feces in yard — the smell may strike you before you actually see them

- ☐ worn track around fence — an indication that the dog is out a lot

- ☐ sleeping or unalert dog — shake fence or make any noise to alert or wake up dog

- ☐ If the dog is tied up and you have to cross its path, don't do so. An aggressive dog may get a burst of strength and break its rope or chain.

- ☐ If the dog is in a yard where an underground electric fence is confining it don't consider that type of fence a valid means of containment. The dog may get a rush of adrenaline and cross the fence line. The dog's state of aggression will numb its body from the shock and it may bite you.

- ☐ *Use your discretion. If your safety is at risk, refuse to deliver the package and explain to your supervisor why you refused to deliver it.*

Vehicles entering the dog owner's yard:

Dogs have learned that a vehicle entering their property signals someone approaching the house. A dog will hear or see the intruder and begin barking, challenging the person and warning him to stay away. The dog often continues barking until the person gets in his vehicle and drives away. When this happens, the dog believes it has done its job by scaring the intruder away. It has won its challenge.

This barking ritual can build an adrenaline high that could make the dog break through a window or door and at worst trigger a bite if the dog gets loose. You will need to be ready to defend yourself against such a dog if this happens. See below for the sections on defensive tactics for dog encounters and attacks.

If a dog continues to bark wildly whenever you drive up, notify the owner of the danger that could result should the dog get loose. If the owner fails to take reasonable measures, such as securing the dog away from windows and doors and making sure the dog is not loose when you arrive, refuse to come to the house.

Why dogs bark at doorbell rings and knocks at the door:

The dog has learned that the doorbell or a knock at the door means someone is on the other side. The dog will bark either because the person is invading its territory or because it is excited about meeting the person. Either way, the dog begins to associate the doorbell or knock with someone arriving. If the dog barks to protect its territory, it will believe it has won once the person leaves, making the dog confident that its bark has scared away the invader. The next time someone knocks or rings the doorbell, the dog will bark more intensely. If the person enters the house, the dog may either continue feeling aggressive about the invader or switch to being friendly because the new person gives it positive attention, touches it and makes friends with it.

If the dog has been barking out of excitement, it learns that when the person comes in, it will be rewarded with a touch and attention. This will make the dog bark more intensely the next time because it gets excited about the idea that the person will enter and give it friendly attention.

If owner is present:

- ☐ Insist the dog be placed in a secure area. Try saying, "I *need* you to put the dog away." If the owner resists, you could try saying, "I would feel better if you would put your dog away."

- ☐ Never pet the dog. You are not part of the dog's social order, and it may bite you even if you have petted it before.

- ☐ Avoid quick movements. The dog could be nervous, and a quick movement will trigger its fear-biting response.

- ☐ If the owner answers the door with the dog or the dog shows up during the meeting and becomes aggressive, prevent the dog from escaping and biting by grasping the door and closing it. If time permits tell the owner: "I need to close the door," or "I need you to close the door, because your dog may bite."

- ☐ If the dog becomes aggressive, don't grasp the owner in an attempt to use her as a shield. The dog may view your actions as an attack on the owner and may bite you to protect her.

When giving something to a person with a dog or taking anything from him:

- ☐ Have the person come to you; this will make the dog invade your space instead of your invading its personal space. A dog may bite you if you invade its space or may perceive your coming towards it as a threat.

- ☐ Have the person take the object while you hold the object close to you; the dog could perceive your hand reaching out as a threat.

- ☐ When leaving, do not turn your back on the dog and walk away. Instead, either walk slowly backwards to a safe distance while always keeping your eye on the dog or allow the owner and dog to leave first.

- ☐ If the dog becomes aggressive at any time, walk backwards to create space and place the object you are trying to give the person somewhere else. Tell the owner to stop coming towards you.

- ☐ If a screen door is the only door between you and the dog and the dog is jumping on it, place your foot and hand on the door to make sure the dog doesn't force it open. If the door is broken shout for the owner and/or spray repellent at the dog through the screen. See below for a discussion of how to use dog repellent spray.

- ☐ Don't give packages to a child or take them from her when a dog is present. Dogs know children are vulnerable and may see them as property which needs protecting. A child can bond so closely to her dog that the dog will instinctively protect her as if the child were its own.

Defensive tactics against a dog encounter:

- ☐ Do not run; you will only cause the dog's biting instinct to surface.

- ☐ If a dog is following you; stop and evaluate. The dog may just want to smell you.

- ☐ Stop and stand sideways, so the dog doesn't think you are challenging it.

- ☐ Avoid quick movement. The dog could be nervous and a quick movement may trigger fear-biting.

- ☐ If the dog is coming towards you, move   backwards and sideways, keeping an eye on the dog. This gives you space and time to react.

- ☐ Carry a high-pitched sound device. See below for how to use the device.

- [ ] Give it some common commands ("stay," "sit," "down"). This makes the dog think maybe you are in charge.

- [ ] Be careful about giving negative commands ("no," "get out of here"). They may work, but if a dog perceives them as a threat you may escalate the dog's aggression and get bitten.

- [ ] Look at the dog, but don't stare into its eyes. Look at the top of its head or at its eyebrows. Looking away may tell the dog it has won the challenge, and it may bite you.

- [ ] If you know the dog, relax it by using its name.

- [ ] Once the dog loses interest in you, move slowly backwards until you are out of its sight.

- [ ] Provide the dog room for an escape by not cutting off escape routes such as a door or gate.

- [ ] Remain calm by taking deep breaths. This will calm your body; dogs can sense tension and fear. If the dog senses your fear (and it probably will), it will gain confidence about biting you.

- [ ] If cornered, remain still and wait until the dog loses interest. This usually takes only a few minutes, so be patient. Then move slowly away.

Defending yourself against a dog attack: stop, drop and curl:

If the attack is imminent, fall on the ground and curl up in a ball, protecting your vital organs, face and ears. Do not scream or yell. This will only make the dog more confident. Its survival instinct will surface, and it will attack with renewed force. Once you are on the ground and silent, you are no longer a threat.

If an attack isn't imminent:

- [ ] Stop and stand sideways, so the dog doesn't think you are challenging it.

- [ ] Evaluate the dog's body language. See "How to understand a dog's body language" at the end of this chapter.

- [ ] If the dog is attacking, present a moving target by waving something in front of the dog. Walk backwards, keeping an eye on the dog.

Don't run or turn your back.

☐ If bitten *don't pull away*. This is very difficult to do, but if you pull away, the bite will be much more serious because the dog will resist having anything pulled from its mouth and will fight harder to hold on, causing more skin-tearing and deeper wounds.

☐ Use defensive options in escalating order: verbal commands, dog repellent spray, striking techniques and stronger measures.

☐ As soon as you can, notify Animal Control or the police.

How to use dog repellent spray:

Whatever brand or type of dog repellent spray you decide to use, read the directions carefully. Check the can regularly to make sure it's still in working order. Do this by shaking the contents vigorously and spraying a small amount. Don't spray too much because repeated testing will use up the spray and leave you with too little when you really need it. If it is cold, make sure the brand you use doesn't freeze. Keep it warm by putting it next to your body.

Dog repellent spray is a nonlethal product that temporarily disorients the dog by surprising it. Dogs don't expect you to reach out and touch them without using your hands. The spray also gives the dog a quick liquid sting and causes temporary eye and nose irritation which distracts it. When it feels the irritation, it will attempt to rub off the substance by pawing at it or rolling on the ground. If you spray the repellent in the dog's mouth, it will immediately begin salivating and be distracted from biting. If the wind is low and the repellent's pressure is at full strength, most sprays can reach up to 12 feet.

In my experience, the spray works on dogs that have not decided to bite but may do so at any time, such as dogs that are circling you or barking at you but not moving. Don't think the spray is your main line of defense. Dogs that are attacking or are intent on biting you may see it as a threat or a challenge, and in their desire to overcome this challenge will become more aggressive. Such dogs are full of adrenaline and may not feel the spray's effects. When using dog repellent spray:

☐ Remember that although you have been told to spray the dog's eyes, that is an almost impossible target to hit. Compared to humans' eyes, dogs have much larger tear ducts and a third eyelid. These assist them in recovering faster. I have been more successful spraying the dog in the mouth. This stimulates the dog's licking reflex, thus stopping it from biting. Also, the mouth is a much larger target.

☐ If the dog is biting you or has its face very close to you, try spraying into its nostrils. This will instantly cause maximum irritation, and the dog will back off.

☐ Spray in a figure eight motion, creating a continuous wall of spray. This will give you a greater chance of hitting some part of the dog's face.

☐ Start spraying as soon as you see the dog coming at you, assuming you have the can out and are ready to use it. You must be ready, because a delay will allow the dog to get too close to you or actually begin biting you.

☐ Walk slowly backwards keeping an eye on the dog. This creates space and gives you time to think about your other options. See below for how to use striking techniques.

☐ Give verbal obedience commands to the dog ("sit," "down" or "stay") as you are walking slowly backwards.

☐ While walking backwards, you are also escaping. Some dogs think they have done their jobs when you have gone away from their territory.

High-pitched sound devices:

These emit a high-pitched tone that humans can't hear but dogs can. The device should be used as soon as the dog encounter becomes threatening. These devices cause discomfort to the dog's hearing but have no negative aftereffects. They are about the size of a garage-door opener and fit in the palm of your hand or clip onto your waistband or belt. When you push the activating button, the dog first becomes surprised because it can't tell where the high-pitched sound is coming from. Then it quickly realizes that as it gets closer to you, the sound gets more intense. Being surprised and disturbed by the sound, the dog may not come any closer to you. This device doesn't work on all dogs, but it is an effective protection against dogs that have not yet decided to bite you but could do so at any moment.

Fighting back an attack using striking techniques:

During an attack or if an attack is imminent, you may decide to use striking techniques. Your objective is to destroy the dog's confidence by striking it with dramatic, instant, painful strikes and to survive the encounter with the least amount of injury to yourself. If you think you can't strike the dog effectively, don't use this option. The dog may view your ineffective strikes as a challenge, which will make it fight even harder, thus increasing your chance of injury.

**Kick or knee
to the chest**

**Punch back of the
neck where the
shoulders meet**

**Punch downward with
forearm to the spine**

**Uppercut to
the throat**

How to use striking techniques:

☐ Knee or kick the dog in the chest; this will knock the wind out of it.

☐ If possible get the dog's attention by moving something over your head; this will get the dog to focus on the moving target and expose its chest.

☐ Punch, chop or strike the back of the neck where the shoulders meet, or aim for the spine. Use any object that will make an impact.

☐ Use your forearm to punch downward on the dog's spine or drive downward with your body weight going to the ground.

☐ Give an upper cut to the throat.

☐ Slam the dog to the ground or up against a wall.

☐ Keep an eye on the dog at all times.

☐ If the dog retreats, walk backwards to an escape route.

Loose dogs and stray dogs (notify Animal Control or the local police):

A loose dog or a stray dog has been allowed to determine its own territory. The dog now believes its roaming area, regardless of the size, belongs to it. This makes the dog unpredictable even if it appears friendly. Anyone invading its territory will make the dog protect it, so stay away from all stray dogs and notify Animal Control or the police.

Dogs trained for protection:

While being trained to protect its owner and her property, the dog has always been allowed to win. Because of this, the dog's confidence has been so strongly built up that it thinks it can overcome anything a human can give out. Be prepared to divert the dog's attention from you to a target object that it can defeat, such as a hat or sack. While it is attacking the object, it will become vulnerable to your repellent spray, striking techniques or stronger measures.

Dogs not trained for protection:

Similar to a dog trained for protection, a dog not specifically trained for protection will still instinctively protect its house or yard as its territory. It believes that it has won all challenges from people invading its space. After all, it scares you and others away when it barks.

Why dogs try to scare off people in uniforms:

If you are wearing a uniform, you need to know why dogs will react to you by barking. A uniformed person enters the dog's yard. It barks; the person leaves. The dog thinks that it has scared them away. Thus, uniformed people who come and go as part of their jobs have indirectly built the dog's confidence in its ability to challenge them. Now the dog perceives anyone wearing a uniform who invades its territory as a threat. This makes the dog potentially dangerous even if it appears friendly.

The treat myth:

If you carry treats to smooth things over with some dogs, the dogs will see people entering their property as a good thing. The problem arises when new delivery personnel or strangers get confused by the approaching dog. The dog is looking for its treat, but the stranger may well think it's about to attack and will hit it, spray it with dog repellent or use even stronger force. Your treats have created a painful, even lethal, trap for the dog.

How to understand a dog's body language:

Study the body language of dogs you encounter during work, as well as your own pets. What makes a dog excited? What makes it fearful? What stresses it? What does your behavior contribute to the dog's behavior? Familiarize yourself with other types of dogs with different temperaments and from different breeds. Notice especially how the different kinds of dogs look when they are experiencing various emotions ranging from excitement and joy to fear and aggressiveness. Before long you will begin anticipating a particular dog's behaviors just by the way it looks, and you will be able to do this for the other types of dogs you have studied.

The dog's eyes are very hard to read. Because they are small, you have to get close up to study them. When the dog is afraid or ready to attack, its eyes glare, even if it is excited about biting you. When the dog is happy or excited in a friendly way, its eyes look soft. When the dog is sick or sad, its eyes look weak.

Below are the most common body language signs associated with the behaviors you need to know about. Once these become recognizable, you should begin to expand your knowledge by learning the mixed signals dogs give because of undesirable genetics, incorrect training and poor environment. Also, dogs' body language varies according to whether or not they have a tail or have prick or floppy ears.

Remember that the dog's body language does not lie. It does not use its body language to trap you into getting bitten. Dogs may be master manipulators when they want their way, but, to our advantage, they do not use manipulation when they intend to attack or bite.

1. Friendly or playful body language:

☐ Total body moving side to side while moving forward in a relaxed way.

☐ Face relaxed while moving.

☐ Mouth opening and closing, relaxed.

☐ Bouncing off the ground with body swinging.

☐ Front legs stretched out forward with rear end in the air so that the dog. appears to be bowing with its whole body wiggling.

Friendly

☐ Moving forward then stopping, while bouncing from side to side.

2. Potentially threatening body language:

☐ Dog's head is turned but it is still looking at you.

☐ Dog is circling you, attempting to attack from behind. *Good time to utilize dog repellent spray or high-pitched sound devices.*

☐ Head is carried high or low — high head shows a dominant dog; low head shows a fearful dog.

☐ Could be barking or silent; it does not matter which.

☐ Mouth is tensed when closed with lips pulled back tight — could be growling.

Potentially threatening

☐ Front legs are stretched out forward with rear end in the air so that the dog appears to be bowing, *but its body is stiff, not moving.*

3. Dangerous body language:

☐ A surge of adrenaline will surface, and the dog's body will stiffen. The stiffness will happen whether the dog is moving or still.

☐ Hackles (hair along the neck and spine) will rise.

☐ Teeth could be showing. Dogs with large muzzle skin will seldom show teeth because they are unable to lift the muzzle skin.

☐ Dog maintains direct eye contact that results in tunnel vision. The dog doesn't get distracted by any other movement around it and is unable to hear its owner's commands.

☐ Dog is barking and not moving, trying to warn you to stay away.

☐ The dog's tail could be wagging because it is happy and excited about biting you. A dog with its tail tucked under may bite you out of fear.

Dangerous

☐ The dog makes a fast, direct approach then stops; its next approach may be to bite you. *Good time to utilize dog repellent spray or high-pitched sound devices.*

Keep in mind:

If the attack is imminent and you are knocked down to the ground, curl up in a protective ball. It is not instinctive for a single, domesticated dog, or dogs without a strong killing instinct, to attack its prey when its prey is motionless. This is the same concept that you may have learned about bear attacks. Usually, neither a bear nor a dog will attack a motionless person or prey. This does not hold true for dogs with a strong killing instinct, however. For a description of how they behave, see the chapter on "Dogs That Are Dangerous or Fighters, Because of Breeding or Learned Behavior."

WITNESSES TO DOG ATTACKS ON PEOPLE AND TO DOG FIGHTS

How to incapacitate a dog that is attacking someone else:

While the following may seem quite violent, you must remember that you may some day experience a dog attack first hand. The attack may be against someone you know and love. Therefore, while it may be difficult to envision ever being able to perform a violent act against a dog, if you ever witness a dog attack, you must know what to do.

1. You can incapacitate a dog that is attacking *when no weapon is available* using the "Wishbone Grasp." Your goal is to stop the attack against the other person and prevent the dog from redirecting its attack to you. Using the "Wishbone Grasp" may immediately stop the attack and will prevent the dog from moving quickly because it dislocates one or both of the dog's hind legs.

- ☐ Approach the dog from behind without making any noise.

- ☐ If you're strong, grasp both of the dog's rear legs by the ankles and pull them toward you as fast as you can, while simultaneously lifting the dog in the air. Then slam the dog down, either onto the ground or any sufficiently large stationary object. If you are not especially strong, try the following methods for stopping the attack.

- ☐ For dogs taller than knee high, grasp one of the dog's rear ankles and lift, while simultaneously falling on the dog's hips with your forearm and continuing to lift the dog's leg straight up.

- ☐ For dogs shorter than knee high, grasp one of the dog's rear ankles and lift, while simultaneously driving your knee downward onto the dog's hips.

Wishbone grasp

Wishbone grasp for dogs taller than knee high

Wishbone grasp for dogs smaller than knee high

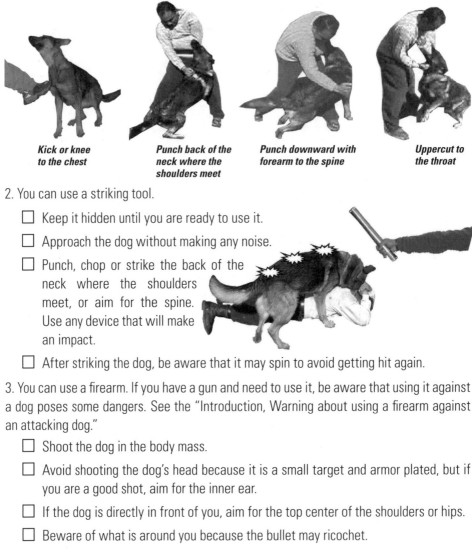

Kick or knee to the chest

Punch back of the neck where the shoulders meet

Punch downward with forearm to the spine

Uppercut to the throat

2. You can use a striking tool.

☐ Keep it hidden until you are ready to use it.

☐ Approach the dog without making any noise.

☐ Punch, chop or strike the back of the neck where the shoulders meet, or aim for the spine. Use any device that will make an impact.

☐ After striking the dog, be aware that it may spin to avoid getting hit again.

3. You can use a firearm. If you have a gun and need to use it, be aware that using it against a dog poses some dangers. See the "Introduction, Warning about using a firearm against an attacking dog."

☐ Shoot the dog in the body mass.

☐ Avoid shooting the dog's head because it is a small target and armor plated, but if you are a good shot, aim for the inner ear.

☐ If the dog is directly in front of you, aim for the top center of the shoulders or hips.

☐ Beware of what is around you because the bullet may ricochet.

If you witness a dog fight, keep these points in mind:

Fighting is a survival instinct that allows dogs to maintain order with the least amount of injury as possible. If the leader male (often called "the alpha") kept fighting to subdue upstart members of the pack until an injury or death occurred, then it would not have any assistants left to help in hunting or in future breeding to keep the pack regenerating. Dogs have mastered the idea of disciplining other dogs just enough to get their point across, and at the same time to give respect to other dogs quickly to avoid a confrontation. Fighting dogs have been bred to ignore this vital survival social skill.

When two ordinary, non-fighting dogs meet each other, they use body language which will help them determine if a challenge is present. In the initial greeting, the dog's body will stiffen, it will stand erect and carry its head higher than normal.

If one of the two doesn't show respect through its body language, then the other will challenge it. A dog gives respect simply by turning and lowering its head or body and/or initiating play.

If another dog makes contact with any part of its body without showing respect, the dog will give a warning growl. If no respect is then given, a fight ensues. This challenge takes one to three seconds. When fully joined in a fight, both dogs are in complete tunnel vision, their bodies filling up with adrenaline. They do not feel most of the pain caused by the fight.

A fight usually lasts no more than ten seconds and sounds a lot worse than it is. Usually the dog that is winning (typically the dog that is on top) will stop, and if the other one is still not showing respect or submission, the fight will continue. For fighting breeds, a fight could last until death.

If a dog fight occurs, you stand a high chance of getting bitten if you're alone and you attempt to break up the fight. The dogs are going to react to any close movement or contact as a threat and will bite whatever gets in their way.

How to prevent a dog fight from starting:

Because almost any dog can get into a fight if challenged or attacked, as a dog owner you should take these precautions.

☐ Spay or neuter your dog. Spaying a female minimizes its protective instincts by controlling its hormones. Neutering a male stops its testosterone from surging when it meets a female in heat, leading to behavior equivalent to a rutting deer sparring for a female.

☐ Be cautious about having your dog meet a strange dog of the same sex because two dogs of the same sex have a greater chance of getting into a fight.

☐ Recognize the body language of a dog's challenge (described in the above section) and stop the fight before it occurs. Do this verbally by saying, "Hey knock it off." Do anything else your dog will respond to, such as a loud distraction. Hit something with your hand or your lead. If you have a leather lead, snap it.

☐ Carry a walking stick or can of dog repellent spray to protect your dog when out for a walk. See below for how to use dog repellent spray.

How to handle the beginning of a dog fight:

☐ If the dogs have begun fighting, approach them in silence. Yelling will only add stress to the fight. Even worse, your dog may turn around and come back to you, making it vulnerable to the other dog and increasing the energy of the fight.

☐ Do not hit any of the dogs. The dog you hit will think either that the pain came from the other dog and thus increase the energy of its fighting, or it will think you caused the pain and, as a reflex, may release the other dog and bite you instead.

☐ Have a tag line on your dog if it has a tendency to start fights. This is a short (two or three inches) piece of cord attached to the ring of a training chain collar. It allows you to grab your dog easily.

How to break up a dog fight:

☐ If your dog is on a lead and you are carrying a walking stick, use the stick to strike the other dog before it gets to your dog. If you have a can of dog repellent with you, spray at the fighting dogs' heads in a figure eight motion.

☐ Grasp the winner, usually the one on top. Once freed, the loser may run away or stop fighting.

☐ If you are weak, allow the dogs to get tired and then enter the battle.

☐ If you have a leash, shirt or towel, wrap it around the aggressor's hind legs and pull towards you. Then start slowly circling. If you grasp one dog and the other dog is still coming at it, release that dog or you will be making it vulnerable to serious injury.

☐ Have another person grasp the other dog by its legs or tail and step away with it.

☐ If the dog is biting and holding on don't pull the dog towards you. Lift it straight up by the collar until the dog releases its hold, telling the dog, "No!" or anything else that might make it release.

☐ Throw a blanket or towel, anything that will go over one or both of the dogs' heads, covering their eyes so they will stop fighting because they can't see or will target something else such as the blanket or towel.

☐ Turn on a water hose and spray directly at the dogs' mouths, filling them with water and forcing them to release.

How to use dog repellent spray:

Whatever brand or type of dog repellent spray you decide to use, read the directions carefully. Check the can regularly to make sure it's still in working order. Do this by shaking the contents vigorously and spraying a small amount. Don't spray too much because repeated testing will use up the spray and leave you with too little when you really need it. If it is cold, make sure the brand you use doesn't freeze. Keep it warm by putting it next to your body.

Dog repellent spray is a nonlethal product that temporarily disorients the dog by surprising it. Dogs don't expect you to reach out and touch them without using your hands. The spray also gives the dog a quick liquid sting and causes temporary eye and nose irritation which distracts it. When it feels the irritation, it will attempt to rub off the substance by pawing at it or rolling on the ground. If you spray the repellent in the dog's mouth, it will immediately begin salivating and be distracted from biting. If the wind is low and the repellent's pressure is at full strength, most sprays can reach up to 12 feet.

In my experience, the spray works on dogs that have not decided to bite but may do so at any time, such as dogs that are circling you or barking at you but not moving. Don't think the spray is your main line of defense. Dogs that are attacking or are intent on biting you may see it as a threat or a challenge, and in their desire to overcome this challenge will become more aggressive. Such dogs are full of adrenaline and may not feel the spray's effects. When using dog repellent spray:

☐ Remember that although you may have been told to spray the dog's eyes, that is an almost impossible target to hit. Compared to humans' eyes, dogs have much larger tear ducts and a third eyelid. These assist them in recovering faster. I have been more successful spraying the dog in the mouth. This stimulates the dog's licking reflex, thus stopping it from biting. Also, the mouth is a much larger target.

☐ Spray the attacking dog's face in a figure eight motion, creating a continuous wall of spray. This will give you a greater chance of hitting some part of its face.

WHAT TO DO
IF YOU ARE ATTACKED
BY A PACK OF DOGS

As wild dogs gradually evolved into the domestic animals we know today, they became close to us humans, but they did not lose all their primitive instincts, especially the one to form a pack and attack prey. When two or more dogs are together, they will form a pack. Domesticated dogs in packs don't attack humans for food. They do attack because of aggressive instincts.

The risk of getting attacked by a pack of dogs is growing because of:

☐ lack of owner responsibility, allowing dogs to roam free.

☐ an overwhelming increase in the pet dog population, including pets that come from fighting breeds. See the chapter on "Dogs That Are Dangerous or Fighters, because of Breeding or Learned Behavior."

☐ uncontrolled breeding practices which lead to dogs' being abandoned.

Any dog can contribute to a pack attack, regardless of its strength, breed, size, age or sex. I have demonstrated this by putting a weak dog in between strong dogs to mirror a pack situation. The weak dog almost immediately becomes equally as strong as its two partners, if not stronger. Some dogs, however, are more likely to become pack leaders and will cause severe damage to humans without having to be stimulated by other dogs.

Dogs in packs attack the same kinds of human victims as the animal prey they would seek out in the wild. These are the young, weak, injured and old. It is rare for a dog or pack to attack a physically fit prey (animal or human), because they hesitate to get injured themselves.

A pack of roaming dogs should cause serious concern. Authorities should take immediate action to remove or split up the pack and hold the dogs' owners accountable for their animals' behavior. Most states have passed laws and ordinances to make sure owners license their dogs and keep them under control and on leash when they are off their property. If owners violate the dog ordinances, they will be fined. For repeated violations, authorities may remove their dogs entirely. Despite these laws, some owners will continue to abandon unwanted dogs along roadsides and in the woods. Some owners will always be too lazy or uninformed to train their dogs. Some will insist that confining their dogs is cruel and will let them roam free unless the dog authorities intervene.

What to do if you are attacked by a pack of dogs:

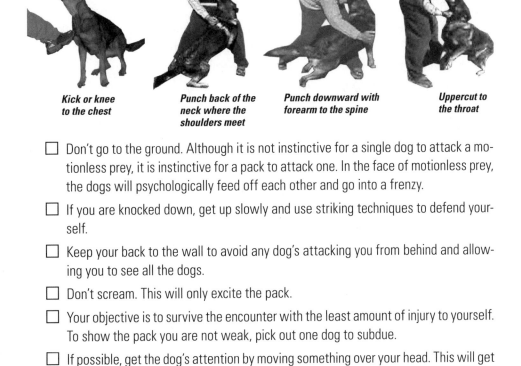

| Kick or knee to the chest | Punch back of the neck where the shoulders meet | Punch downward with forearm to the spine | Uppercut to the throat |

☐ Don't go to the ground. Although it is not instinctive for a single dog to attack a motionless prey, it is instinctive for a pack to attack one. In the face of motionless prey, the dogs will psychologically feed off each other and go into a frenzy.

☐ If you are knocked down, get up slowly and use striking techniques to defend yourself.

☐ Keep your back to the wall to avoid any dog's attacking you from behind and allowing you to see all the dogs.

☐ Don't scream. This will only excite the pack.

☐ Your objective is to survive the encounter with the least amount of injury to yourself. To show the pack you are not weak, pick out one dog to subdue.

☐ If possible, get the dog's attention by moving something over your head. This will get the dog to focus on the moving target and expose its chest.

☐ Knee or kick the dog in the chest; this will knock the wind out of it.

☐ Move slowly, using dynamic striking techniques such as a punch, chop or blow to the back of the dog's neck where the shoulders meet, or aim for the spine.

☐ Give an upper cut to the throat.

☐ Keep an eye on the dog at all times.

☐ If the dog retreats, walk slowly backwards to an escape route.

Key points to remember during a dog pack attack:

☐ If your own dog is with you, it may become so excited it will forget you are its friend and master. You should consider it an enemy during a pack attack because its pack instinct may become so strong that it might attack you.

☐ As mentioned above, single a dog out to strike, preferably the smallest and weakest one. This will show the other pack members how strong you are. Charge after the one you've chosen, using striking techniques, as described above.

☐ Get up on a high obstacle such as a tree or the top of a car, roof or table. The dogs may continue attacking, but being out of their reach may give you the extra time you need to think or attract attention from passers by.

☐ Go into a pond, lake or river, if one is nearby. Move slowly into it. Dogs are weakest in water and are unable to circle you, enabling you to keep an eye on them all the time.

☐ Get a large obstacle between you and the dogs, moving it when one approaches, or if you are able, swinging it at them.

☐ If you have a striking tool or weapon, target the dog's body mass, back, spine and legs. Avoid the head. It is a small target and armor-plated.

☐ As soon as possible notify Animal Control or the police.

DOGS THAT ARE DANGEROUS OR FIGHTERS, BECAUSE OF BREEDING OR LEARNED BEHAVIOR

Where did fighting breeds come from?

Because of the survival instincts that come from their primitive origins, all dogs can become dangerous at any given time. However, certain dogs have been selectively bred to be mentally and physically stronger than others. The majority came originally from Asia. To increase the breed's ability to produce fighting dogs or high-level guard and protection dogs, breeders on this continent and elsewhere bred selectively to make changes in the dog's body. These included a thicker and looser skin, stronger jaw muscles, thicker and longer hair, and a stronger neck. Dogs bred this way were used to fight each other for profit, hunt large game, kill the enemy in wartime, and fight large game for profit, a "sport" called baiting.

The bite of a dog with these strong fighting attributes is immensely powerful, compared to the normal dog. A German Shepherd's bite (a dog not bred for strength in fighting) versus a Pit Bull's bite would cause less damage. The German Shepherd's muzzle is long and produces a long bite, as opposed to the smaller muzzle on Pit Bulls and other fighting breeds which exert a compact pressure on a smaller area, causing tearing and doing far more damage than does a German Shepherd. Police K-9 trainers know this and will not use these types of dogs for protection. Their main goal is to detain criminals and allow the courts to decide their punishment. Damages could be awarded to the criminal if the Police K-9 Unit violated the section of the U.S. Constitution's Eighth Amendment that bans inflicting "cruel and unusual punishments." They also know that human error is always present, and an error made while using a dog with such a strong bite would cost the taxpayers a lot of money in legal damages.

The inconsistency of temperament in fighting breed dogs:

The temperaments of individual dogs in the fighting breeds are inconsistent in countries that don't practice selective breeding. This stems from not understanding and not testing the breed's temperament standard and from cross-breeding them with dogs that have the attributes for being good pets. This dilution in breeding causes confusion. You may get both pet quality dogs and some very strong fighters in the same litter.

In the United States, we keep all dogs whether or not they fit the breed standard. In other countries where selective breeding is practiced and dogs are used for their true purposes, breeders will neuter or euthanize a puppy or dog which does not meet the standard, thus stopping it from transferring its undesirable genetics.

Unethical breeding practices, cross-breeding and not understanding the dog's genetic makeup cause confusion about the fighting dog's true temperament. Such a dog may become aggressive at any time even if it has been socialized with humans or other dogs. Just because the dog has remained passive as it matured is no indication that it won't some day exhibit the traits of its breed. The dog may never have been in a situation which required its fighting instincts to surface. But when and if it is challenged by another dog or a human, or it perceives a threat, the dog can unexpectedly show its true purpose in life and cause serious injury to whomever challenged or threatened it.

Even though the dog is primarily a fighting dog that only attacks other dogs, it still has instincts that could cause it to feel challenged or threatened by humans. See the chapter for "Parents," the section on "Nine kinds of aggressive behaviors."

Loyalty in fighting dogs:

All the attributes that make the fighting dog dangerous can also work to your advantage. You must know the dog's limitations and weaknesses. You may not always be able to guard against the danger of your dog's biting someone, so you must be prepared to be responsible for the financial cost and psychological long-term stress if a bite occurs. These dogs are very loyal to their own family's social order. The fighting breeds will defend you from an attack by a human or dog with the same amount of fearlessness they show when fighting for sport or in wartime. They are natural born protectors with the strength of an army.

Body language of a fighting / dangerous dog:

Fighting dogs have been bred to not display any signs of aggression prior to a fight or attack. This makes them silent attackers. In illegal dog fighting rings, the handlers will introduce the dogs to each other, called facing them, getting them ready to fight. If one of the fighters makes any noise prior to the fight, it is declared the loser. The silent attacker has been bred for maximum stealth, so its opponent doesn't know when the attack is coming, and the dog doesn't waste any unnecessary energy.

When a bite victim claims the dog never made any noise and never acted like it was going to attack her, that person was bitten by a silent attacker. The dog did what it was supposed to do — not make any noise, just attack. This is just one reason such dogs are dangerous.

Killing and fighting instinct:

Any dog can have a killing instinct. However, it is more prevalent in fighting breeds that have been bred to have this behavior take over when they are faced with aggression or stress. Once the dog is faced with another dog, its killing instinct surfaces. During the fight or kill, the dog's body automatically gets a rush of adrenaline which numbs its pain and makes it fight more intensely. Once it makes contact with its opponent, it will shake its victim vigorously in order to tear and puncture the skin. Tunnel vision surfaces, and the dog is unable to hear or think of anything other than fighting or killing. The dog will refuse to release its target even if the target is motionless. Anyone who attempts to intervene must take drastic measures, such as prying the attacker's mouth open with a thick wooden stick or metal bar, called a breaking stick. Remember, this dog is using the same inbred attribute that makes it a successful fighter and killer.

How to identify the killing instinct:

You can tell if your dog has the killing instinct by watching it interact and play with toys and other animals. If your dog goes after its toy, shaking it vigorously and refusing to let go, or if it is successful in catching a small animal and shakes it to kill it instead of just playing with it, then I would believe it has the killing instinct, and you should be concerned about it. The chase or retrieving is not a sign of the killing instinct. For a dog that has the killing instinct, the chase may be the start of the kill. What it does after it catches its prey would tell you whether or not the dog has the killing instinct. For example, if the dog bites a motionless target or animal then continues to shake it vigorously, maintaining a tight hold, it has the killing instinct.

How humans contribute to the killing instinct:

- ☐ rough playing with the dog (see below for how rough playing stimulates aggression)
- ☐ playing tug-of-war (This teaches the dog to pull in the same way it would to take down its prey and tear meat from it. It is the worst thing you can do to reinforce a dog's killing instinct.)
- ☐ allowing the dog to roam free, claiming its territory
- ☐ having no obedience training or using the wrong method, making the dog unable to control its impulses and instincts
- ☐ not channeling the dog's instincts through another activity, such as fetching, swimming or tracking.

The deadliest sin an owner of a fighting dog can commit:

Training the dog to bite a motionless object is the worst thing you can do! The dog is told to bite on a hanging tire or a rag. While it's biting this object, the handler either pulls the dog up or allows it to jump and hang off its feet for long periods of time. This kind of training teaches the dog to connect the biting to killing on motionless objects. This is why becoming motionless will not protect you from a dog bred or trained to fight or that is dangerous.

How rough playing affects dominant and dangerous dogs:

1. *Dog-to-dog rough playing*: To raise the ultimate fighting dog, owners will pick the puppy that consistently beats its litter mates in challenges for food and in rough play-fighting. This is usually the strongest pup in the litter. As the dog matures, the owner has it continue rough playing with other dogs, making sure that it wins and thus building its confidence for the real fighting ahead. Rough playing teaches the dog mock fighting. If the dog is allowed to win these play fights and dominate other, weaker dogs,  it will begin to believe it can win any fight. The weaker, defeated dogs against which it fights will learn to fear dominant dogs and will show bursts of aggression against other dogs. These fearful dogs become dangerous because they will attack other dogs without provocation or warning. Their fear has made them into silent attackers.

2. *Dog-to-human rough playing*: Through rough play with humans a dominant dog learns how to bite people and discovers that they give up when it bites harder. Because humans usually employ their hands and feet when rough playing with a dog, the dog quickly learns what to target when a real attack or fight is imminent. Rough playing with a human has made it believe it is a winner. The human, however, gets angry when the dog bites too hard during rough play and disciplines the dog, sometimes severely. Now the dog who thought it was a winner gets confused and thinks, "One minute this human was playing with me very nicely and the next minute she starts hitting me." Such confusion breeds fear, and the dog will start having bursts of aggression against humans. It now fears that all humans will try to dominate it and then discipline it for fighting back. This is especially true for dogs from fighting breeds or those that are naturally dominant. Such dogs will take their aggression further than other dogs, attacking humans without provocation or warning. These dogs are like loaded guns with the safety off.

The dog's purpose in life is to serve us:

Our selection of the type of dog we want should not be influenced by its looks, but by understanding the dog's true purpose in life and temperament. Someone selecting a dog must know what is inside the dog's mind before deciding to buy or adopt it. In the U.S., we categorize dogs based on their purpose to serve humans. These categories are listed below, with a brief description of the kind of service they are bred for. Understanding what a dog's purpose is allows us to understand the potential for it to have instincts that could be dangerous or unacceptable to our way of living.

Some inbred purposes require certain breeds of dogs to make contact with and kill their prey if necessary. Some breeds will naturally just chase and corner prey. Some breeds of dogs will by nature serve as companions. Others will perform specific jobs. For a list of these see below for the descriptions in the American Kennel Club breed groups.

In the dog fighting world, however, any naturally aggressive dog *can be made to become a fighter.* All dogs have the instinct to protect themselves, and aggressive dogs have it more strongly.

Why wolves and wolf hybrids should not be made into pets:

Wolves are predators by nature; they can survive alone or with a pack. They are opportunists and scavengers. They target small prey for their survival. Like any other wild animal, they have a natural instinct to fear danger. If they perceive the danger is directed at them and they feel cornered, they will have no choice but to protect themselves by biting.

Wolves communicate more dramatically than the domesticated dog through their body language and their vocal skills in growling, howling and barking. Their movements are more exaggerated. Their voices are pitched higher and louder, and they use them more frequently than do domesticated dogs.

A wolf hybrid comes from a domesticated dog that has been bred with a wolf. If you produce such a hybrid, you will have no idea which genes will dominate any particular hybrid puppy. Within the same litter, hybrid puppies can differ dramatically.

The wolf is far more fearful than a dog, because its survival instincts have not been watered down by hundreds of years of domestication. Its fear makes the dog unpredictable. Whenever the wolf or hybrid perceives something as fearful, its survival instincts can be triggered, and it may bite.

People will attempt to imprint hundreds of years of domestication by socializing wolves or hybrids. This only creates a false sense of security that the wolf or hybrid is a good pet. By socializing wolves or hybrids, you make them comfortable with their surroundings, but you will not remove their predatory and survival instincts. Trying to domesticate a wolf or wolf hybrid by interacting with it and feeding it doesn't stop it from being fearful of strangers outside its perceived pack (you and the other humans who have socialized it), nor will it stop its instinct to kill prey for food.

When added to a family with children or socialized with children outside of their family pack, the wolf or wolf hybrid instinctively adopts behaviors to assert "who is the leader" in its pecking order. In the wild, the wolf constantly tests other pack members in its pecking order, waiting for one of them to show a weakness so it can jump one level higher in rank. Also sometimes it challenges its leader to get the alpha status (the number one dog). It will challenge each pack member through aggressive body language and behavior.

When socialized with humans, the human asserts his leadership position, and the wolf or hybrid knows how to behave. But once the human leader leaves the wolf or hybrid, challenging behaviors take place. Children are small and appear vulnerable and are the first to be challenged. They scream, run like prey and don't know what's dangerous in an animal's behavior. The wolf or hybrid interprets the screams as distress signals from vulnerable prey and will challenge and at worst attack. Children's inability to understand what a threat is through body language makes them even more vulnerable to be challenged and attacked.

Further, the wolf's minimal ability to be trained because it is fearful or feels dominated makes a poor basis for its becoming a good pet. As with dogs, obedience is not instinctive for a wolf. It must be taught to control its behaviors and instincts, but for wolves and hybrids this causes confusion about what their purpose in life is. When people try to domesticate them, they commonly exhibit destructive behavior. So-called "domesticated" wolves and hybrids have no outlet for the instincts that serve them so well in the wild, and they have to find other means of releasing their energies. Their new outlets all too often become destroying things and escaping from confinement so they can run free as they were meant to do.

American Kennel Club purebred, breed group descriptions:

Terriers: are ground hunters. They were bred to hunt and kill vermin. More than any other group, terriers have the ability to display signs of the killing instinct.

Hounds: are hunters that use their vision and sense of smell to find their prey. They have been bred to bark when they have cornered their prey and wait until the human hunter shows up. In addition to their hunting ability, hounds may develop the killing instinct if not trained to control themselves while hunting.

Non-sporting dogs: are a mixture of dogs that don't fit in the other groups. Some have a history of being used for dog fighting or crossed to make a fighting dog. The Bulldog, Chow Chow, Shiba Inu and the Chinese Shar-Pei are in this group.

Herding dogs: have the ability to control many animals at a time over a long distance, guiding them by biting them to gain respect and control. This group could cross the line to reveal the killing instinct, so obedience training is imperative.

Working dogs: do useful work, either independently or with their master. Some have protective guarding instincts while others perform a particular task, such as pulling carts or finding and rescuing people. All of them are very strong. Some of them also have a history of dog fighting and may have the killing instinct. The Akita has a history of fighting in Japan, while the Mastiff, Boxer, Rottweiler and Great Dane were crossed with other dog-fighting breeds to improve their fighting ability.

Sporting dogs: love water and serve the hunter through locating the prey and/or retrieving it if necessary. Dogs in this group may become aggressive if their hunting instinct is not replaced by another job. If not trained to redirect their hunting instinct, sporting dogs become edgy and unpredictable. They seldom exhibit the killing instinct, however.

Toy dogs: are all small. While some should be in the terrier, hound and sporting group, they where placed in this group because of their size. They serve as companions and, in my opinion, make the best watch dogs. They are the easiest dog to maintain, but the hardest for people to remember that they are dogs, not toys. Because of their size, toy dogs make us think we should spoil them, treating them like babies. This unconscious human behavior confuses the dog and starts a chain of behavior problems. Their bite will cause damage, but it won't cause so much damage as to kill a human. Some have the killing instinct and may be the leaders in a pack because of their strong body language and confidence.

Fighting breeds around the world:

The most popular breeds for fighting have originated in Asia. Some of them are recognized by the American Kennel Club and the United Kennel Club, the two most popular dog registries in the United States. Just because they are not performing the task that they were originally bred for doesn't mean that their breed instincts have been removed. Furthermore, it is easy to import fighting breeds not recognized by the two U.S. breed registries. In the future, they will become part of this country's breeding mix, either as purebreds or cross-breeds.

Here is a listing of some of the more commonly seen fighting breeds, which come from all over the world. Some of these breeds are currently present in the United States: Ainu Ken, Akita, American Pit Bull Terrier, American Staffordshire Terrier, Bandog, Bulldog, Bull Terrier, Chin, Chow Chow, Dogue de Bordeaux, Fila, Japanese Spitz, Kai Ken, Kishu Ken, Neapolitan Mastiff, Nippon Terrier, Olde Bulldogge, Shar-Pei, Shiba Inu, Shikoku Ken, Staffordshire Bull Terrier, Tosa Inu.

I N D E X

PICTURE INDEX